BORN AGAIN
Having a Personal Relationship with
God

CHARLES W MORRIS

RSI
PUBLISHING

Copyright © 2021 Charles W Morris
All rights reserved. No part of this book may be used or reproduced by any means, graphic, electronic, or mechanical, including photocopying, recording, taping, or by any information storage retrieval system without the written permission of the publisher except in the case of brief quotations embodied in critical articles and reviews.

Scriptures are taken from the English Standard Version of the Bible

Books may be ordered through booksellers or by contacting:

RSIP Raising the Standard International Publishing L. L. C.

RSIP-Charles Morris
https://www.rsiministry.com
Navarre, Florida

ISBN: 9781955830188
Printed in the United States of America
Edition Date: July 2021

DEDICATION

Acts 20:20-21 ESV how I did not shrink from declaring to you anything that was profitable, and teaching you in public and from house to house, (21) testifying both to Jews and to Greeks of repentance toward God and of faith in our Lord Jesus Christ.

I dedicate this book to all who are seeking after God, to know Him personally. I also dedicate this book to all of those who are faithful witnesses of the faith in them. May the Father honor your faithfulness with much fruit.

CONTENTS

Acknowledgments

Section 1: Examining Ourselves To Guarantee We Are In The Faith

1	Introduction	1
2	Examining Ourselves	5
3	Evidence that the Holy Spirit is Beside Me	12
4	The Three Shreds Of Evidence Proving That The Holy Spirit Is Convicting Us	16
5	The Measuring Tool	25

Section 2: The Five Shreds Of Evidence Of Salvation — 30

6	The First Witness: The Scriptural Testimony	31
7	The Second Witness: The Internal Witness	44
8	The Third Witness: The External Witness	48
9	The Fourth Witness: The Fraternal Witness	61
10	The Fifth Witness: The Paternal Witness	67

Section 3: The Fruit Of The Holy Spirit — 74

11	The Fruit Of The Holy Spirit	75

	Section 4: God's Master Plan Of Salvation	91
12	How To Become A Christian	92
13	The Master Plan Of Evangelism	100
14	Recap of the Five Witnesses of Salvation	113
	About the Author	116

ACKNOWLEDGMENTS

First and foremost, all thanks must go to the Lord Jesus Christ for helping me accomplish this work. To Him be the glory. Throughout many years of ministry, the Lord has used exceptional men and women of God to teach and speak the truth, which I had the honor to hear and receive. These Godly men and women have challenged and modeled the Spirit-filled life for everyone to see and thirst after.

We all should be grateful for the Godly people who left their mark in our hearts and mind. Through their example, we see and experience the need to build mature spiritual fathers and mothers of the faith. Thank you, each one of you that God used to form this book "Born Again."

SECTION 1

EXAMINING OURSELVES TO GUARANTEE WE ARE IN THE FAITH

Chapter 1
INTRODUCTION

This book is about the reality of an authentic experience and personal relationship with God through the Lord Jesus Christ. Developing and having an ongoing personal relationship with God is the most critical activity of human existence. We cannot engage God the Father except through the Son, and we cannot know the Son except through the Person of the Holy Spirit, revealing Him to us. True salvation is more than a "pray this prayer" encounter. True salvation is a "life-changing" experience connected with a "life-giving" God. Thus, the term "Born again."

Salvation starts with a wooing process as the Father calls us to His heart. It is the Holy Spirit that brings about that wooing or conviction upon our hearts that reveals our need for salvation and to develop a relationship with God. When we are lost and under conviction, we may not know that it is God at work calling our heart to His. Many believers are Christians for years before realizing the exuberant vibrancy of the Holy Spirit's presence in and through them. A challenge is issued for those reading and studying this book to be genuinely open to the leadership of the Holy Spirit and God's Word. In that openness, see the work of the Holy Spirit in drawing a heart to the Father.

The Bible was not written by men who were inspired by the Holy Spirit to stimulate theological discussions concerning the ministry and work of the Holy Spirit. The Bible was written and given to us to change men's lives by inspiring a desire for a proper relationship with God the Father, God the Son, and God the Spirit. We need to search the Scriptures concerning the doctrine of salvation and the doctrine of the Holy Spirit and compare it to our own limited personal experiences and limited understanding. We may discover more about being saved and about the Holy Spirit than we can define in a mere doctrinal statement.

People typically have an intense desire to quarrel in theological debates. The arguments are not always theologically based in that they are typically more emotionally bias than biblically founded. Therefore, the correctness of one's doctrine is argued typically from the biased opinion based upon what denominational slant the opponents in the debate lean. The desire to win the controversy stems from the same desire as rooting for a sports team. No one wants to be a part of a losing team. Who wants to walk away from a conversation with a new revelation that the Biblical doctrine they have embraced for decades is false or incomplete? This denominational bias typically leads us to seek and fellowship with people who "believe as we do" so we can have validation for our belief system. Like as some folks have put it, "birds of the same feather flock together.

This self and group validation method of "birds of the same feather, flock together" has been one of the causes of misunderstanding, confusion, and abuse among many within the faith concerning the work, ministry, and Person of the Holy Spirit, especially in developing a relationship with God. Think about the doctrine of salvation for a moment. People can claim they are saved and call themselves Christians, and we have the mindset that we are under obligation to take their word for it without any right to question their faith or confession.

However, what will we do with the fact that our Lord Jesus Christ Himself said that "we shall know them by their fruit?" Know who? We will know the true believer from the false one by their fruit. We will know the Christian who has had an authentic experience of the heart by faith in our Lord Jesus Christ versus the one who only has a confession of the mouth. However, how would we know? What are the witnesses or pieces of evidence of salvation? There is an old saying that says, "The proof is in the pudding." The prayer is that this book will help clear up some of the misconceptions that have plagued the church concerning the work of the Holy Spirit in the salvation process and the evidence that proves someone is genuine in their "born again" experience. It is essential that what we have developed is indeed a relationship with God and not mere religion. If we have spent any time in church at all, we have come to know some who love their religion, denomination, and church, building more than a love relationship with the heavenly Father.

The Holy Spirit's work in the life of both the lost and saved person has been an interest since becoming a believer in 1974. Like most people, when first saved, there was a bombardment of fabricated traditional teachings, emotionally charged convictions, and doctrines based on nothing more than personal experiences and a false belief system. Many "well-meaning" believers poured their time and life out in the hope of seeing this author grow in faith and understanding. However, much of what they taught was nothing more than an echo of half-truths and misunderstandings taught to them.

This book is a Biblical approach to understanding how to develop and have a relationship with God. One key element to this aim is to examine our salvation experience. We do this by the five witnesses, pieces of evidence or proofs of salvation, and the work of the Holy Spirit regarding both pre-salvation and post-salvation conviction and position.

The five witnesses or proofs of true Biblical salvation or being born again are as follows.

1. The Biblical Testimony Witness (Confession)
2. The Spirit Witness (Internal)
3. The Fruit Witness (External)
4. The Fraternal Witness (Brotherly)
5. The Paternal Witness (Fatherly)

Let us join in unity together in this journey of discovering the abundant Spirit-filled life as we uncover the five pieces of evidence, proofs, or witnesses of true salvation.

Chapter 2
EXAMINING OURSELVES

Trusting in the Word of God, and in what it says as being true, is an essential act of faith for the believer because the Word of God is our ultimate source of authority. This book will ask and answer some of the hard questions about developing a relationship with God. This question-and-answer time will help us witness to others concerning the work of the cross and the redemption purchased by our Lord Jesus Christ and in examining those who claim to be Christian brothers and sisters of the faith yet lack the fruit as evidence. Remember that the Word tells us that many will come as wolves in sheep's clothing.

Let us join in unity together in this journey of discovering the abundant Spirit-filled life as we uncover the five pieces of evidence, proofs, or witnesses of true salvation. We will learn how to be "born again," develop, have, and maintain a personal relationship with God.

> *Matthew 7:15 ESV "Beware of false prophets, who come to you in sheep's clothing but inwardly are ravenous wolves.*
>
> *Acts 20:28-30 ESV Pay careful attention to yourselves and to all the flock, in which the Holy Spirit has made you overseers, to care for the church of God, which he obtained with his own blood. (29) I know that after my departure fierce wolves will come in among you, not sparing the flock; (30) and from among your own selves will arise men speaking twisted things, to draw away the disciples after them.*

To discern these wolves in sheep's clothing, we need to know how to be fruit inspectors. We need to examine those who claim to be born again and a part of the body of Christ. However, we always start by examining ourselves as the Apostle Paul said that he did.

> ***2 Corinthians 13:5 ESV Examine yourselves, to see whether you are in the faith. Test yourselves. Or do you not realize this about yourselves, that Jesus Christ is in you?—unless indeed you fail to meet the test!***

To get into the meat of this study, we will need first to lay a foundation in which to build. First, we need to lay out the simple truth about the salvation made available to all of us by God the Father and purchased by our Lord Jesus Christ with His death on the cross and resurrection from the dead. To examine ourselves to ensure that we have experienced and embraced this wonderful gift of salvation, we need to ask ourselves these questions.

- ◊ How do we know that the Holy Spirit is beside us, dealing with us and calling us to God's salvation? What are the pieces of evidence or proof that the Holy Spirit is beside us?

- ◊ How do we know that we have been born again, experienced true Biblical redemption, and have the Holy Spirit within us? What is the evidence or fruit that we are saved and have the Holy Spirit within us other than us saying that we have experienced salvation? How do we know we are developing a relationship with God versus being committed to religion and the things of God? Is there fruit that we and others can examine?

These questions have been some of the motivations for this book on the evidence of an authentic salvation experience. There is great hope that in answering these questions, they will educate the body of Christ over her misunderstanding about the doctrine of salvation and relating to our heavenly Father.

These questions are by no means an attempt to cause someone to doubt their salvation or "born again" experience. The opposite is exact. Questions are a way to examine one's life to solidify with a firm assurance the faith and hope within us. Suppose all we have is our verbal testimony that we have experienced salvation. What happens when trials, periods of indifference, spiritual coldness, or sin cause the oral testimony to grow silent? Where can we go to prove that we are blood-bought, heaven-bound, and precious children of God? Alternatively, is our faith built upon and held up by a religious ceremony of "just pray this prayer to be saved?" Do we have to go back to a one-time event and say that it is proof of our salvation, or can we look over our entire Christian life and see pieces of evidence proving that we are children of God and have an ongoing relationship with God?

This book is in no way a complete study on the ministry, work, and Person of the Holy Spirit, drawing someone to salvation. We certainly cannot cover every facet and specific point or truth on this subject in this small book. Every attempt to accurately outline the precepts needed to understand the evidence or proofs of a salvation experience is noted. There is something innately inadequate in anyone's attempt to explain the grace of God at work in the life of an individual. God's saving grace is marvelous, glorious, and eternal. The mere words of man will fall short in attempting to explain God's nature and character. To think that God would give His eternal Son on a cross to die so that we could be eternally redeemed is somewhat overwhelming.

After having read "BORN AGAIN," we face the decision of being an echo or a voice. The Biblical principles taught must be applied as a solid foundational covenant contract, or they will become just another set of truths that passed through our mind with a "take it or leave it attitude." If they are just intellectual thoughts to have a conversation with others about, we become nothing more than an echo of another man's illumination and revelation. If the truths are internalized and walked out, we become a voice for God and His glorious salvation to the nations. Our Lord said in John 10:10 that He came to give us abundant life, not just life.

*John 10:10 ESV **The thief comes only to steal and kill and destroy. I came that they may have life and have it abundantly.***

In this book, my prayer is that we all will find a new dimension of living in the glorious presence of the Holy Spirit, which dwells within each believer. Furthermore, may we all develop an ongoing personal relationship with God that grows in grace daily. Let us pray together that we will find an abundant life where God's Word is fresh and exciting to our soul, and we experience it in living color. This book is about victory. Yes, victory! It is not a victory residing in the afterlife once we die. It is not about a victory that is only in theory or a victory that gives false hope. It is certainly not a victory chanted in our churches like a cheer at a pep rally, hoping to incite the crowds. It is a now victory that resides in the King of Glory.

The certainty of our faith is a victory that is a "new and now reality" in the fact that we can know that we know that we are children of God, blood-bought, forgiven, and heaven-bound. The Holy Spirit, Divine with infinite majesty, unlimited in glory, pure in holiness, and creative in power, has taken ownership and residence within the believer. The thought that the Divine sovereignty of the Person of the Holy Spirit with all His Glory choosing to dwell within us and desiring to use us to glorify the Father should overwhelm and humble us. Our Lord called it in the Gospel of John "The Abundant Life," but Paul called it in Ephesians "The Spirit-Filled Life."

My life, like many reading this book, was a mess. In early 1974, there was a sense of conviction for about six months as the Lord worked on and led me to salvation. The word "conviction" means to feel or sense a drawing in our thoughts and emotions that something is morally and spiritually wrong and that there is more to life than the consumption of things seeking to satisfy ourselves. There was this overwhelming awareness of spiritual and eternal matters that seemed to dictate the thoughts of every waking moment.

The Holy Spirit was wooing and calling me to the Son of God and the Father to experience a "born again" encounter. Of course, we seldom know what is going on except that we know something different is happening. Therefore, many of us think we are just messed up and need a change of some kind, but unaware of what it looks like and how it could happen. The thought came that if victory over addictions, such as drugs and alcohol, then life would be okay. However, no matter how hard the attempt was to "straighten" up this broken and lonely life, it seemed that it was a move from one mess to another.

Redemption from the Lord Jesus Christ happened when this author received salvation on a Wednesday night,

September 4, 1974, at 1 am. The Holy Spirit invaded our dorm room, and there was a conviction and convincing of sin and the need for a Savior. Then an unexpected change took place. At the time, a life heavily influenced by drugs dominated most activities and money, having not been in a drug-free status for over two years. The life of drug addiction had taken its toll as body weight steadily decreased to 145 pounds, and I was told that I resembled the walking dead. That night under the conviction of the Holy Spirit, for the first time, there was the realization that we are all sinners, we are all lost, and without Christ, we are all going to spend eternity in hell.

This conviction was the wooing of the Holy Spirit as He was calling this heart to the Father. Having dropped to the floor on bended knees, this author cried out to the Lord Jesus Christ to forgive and save. The Holy Spirit moved from the position of being "beside me" to the position of being "within me," and this broken, busted, wounded life became spiritually alive and spiritually healed. There was an exchange of lives having given God this physically, emotionally, and mentally busted self, and then God flooded this heart with His life. The Word of God says that at the point of salvation, our heart becomes the tabernacle or dwelling place of the Father. All this young man knew was that a radical salvation event just happened with the result of having forgiveness of sins, broken strongholds, a relationship with God developed, and a new home in heaven established.

However, how do we know it was authentic and genuine the day or night we called upon Jesus to save us? How do we know that we did not just have an emotional experience while seeking and desiring a life change? How do we know that what happened that day or night was more than us having a drug-induced, alcohol-induced, or emotional meltdown experience? If our experience occurred during church service, how do we know our experience of walking an aisle to pray with the pastor was real? Do not get this wrong. We know we were sincere, but how can we be sure that we have more than emotional sincerity?

Back in Sept. 1974, one work colleague told everyone I had an emotional meltdown and that things would return to normal routine in a few weeks. In other words, the colleague was saying that there would be no long-standing change and that the drug and alcohol addiction would return. How could this author or any true believer prove that our experience with God was more than a moment of emotional trauma trying to find help in anything we could grab or any crutch we could lean on? How can we prove that what we had in Christ was much more than an exchange of one mental and emotional crutch for another? How can we prove that the prayer we cried out to God was mixed with a heart of faith that brought about true Biblical salvation and not just words of desperation, mental ascent, and false religious hope?

The two positions of the Holy Spirit we will cover in "BORN AGAIN" are having the Holy Spirit beside us and having the Holy Spirit within us. Each of these two positions carries pieces of evidence or proof on which we can "hang our hats on." Join in this study as we examine and answer the question, "Are we truly saved, redeemed, and BORN AGAIN?" Do we have a personal relationship with God? By examining our faith and our salvation experience using the five Biblical shreds of evidence of salvation, we can answer these questions and more.

Chapter 3
EVIDENCE THAT THE HOLY SPIRIT IS BESIDE ME.

As we examine the Holy Spirit's work of conviction and salvation, there must be a way to know that we know that we possess more than an emotional experience whereby we prayed to receive our Lord Jesus Christ. People may say, "we know we are saved and have a relationship with God because we pray every day to Him." Of course, the obvious question would be, "do we hear Him answer?" Is the heavenly Father speaking to us like a father to a son? There must be some way to measure the working of the Holy Spirit in the salvation process other than our testimony, experiences, religious experiences, or lack of experiences.

Cars have many measuring tools in them for our convenience and safety. Not only can we know the temperature of our engine to ensure safety, but we can know the temperature inside the car for our maximum comfort. Not only can we know our driving speed to ensure safety and obedience to the established driving laws, but we can also know how long it will take to drive to our next destination.

In the medical field, there was a time when we had to go to the doctor to have our blood pressure or blood sugar checked. Today many families have monitoring machines to check their blood pressure or blood sugar in the convenience of their own homes. The ability to check blood pressure and blood sugar levels in the privacy of our homes gives consumer convenience to the public. This technology also provides us with the ability for daily self-examination to ensure our physical safety.

We are used to measuring many things in our daily lives, but somewhere along the way, we have neglected to use the measuring tools God has given us to evaluate our lives to ensure we are in maximum working order. Even the Apostle Paul said that we should examine ourselves to prove that we are in the faith. Paul also tells us that we need to examine ourselves before taking the "Lord's supper."

> *2 Corinthians 13:5 ESV Examine yourselves, to see whether you are in the faith. Test yourselves. Or do you not realize this about yourselves, that Jesus Christ is in you?—unless indeed you fail to meet the test!*
>
> *1 Corinthians 11:28 ESV Let a person examine himself, then, and so eat of the bread and drink of the cup.*
>
> *1 Corinthians 11:31 ESV But if we judged ourselves truly, we would not be judged.*

Examining ourselves is not a new idea. In the Old Testament, the early patriarchs were to search, try, and consider their ways. The things which God called them to do, He also requires with us.

> *Lamentations 3:40 ESV Let us test and examine our ways, and return to the LORD!*
>
> *Haggai 1:5 ESV Now, therefore, thus says the LORD of hosts: Consider your ways.*

This book is an intense study about being Born Again and developing a personal relationship with God, the Father.

We are to examine ourselves and search out our hearts, and we should ask the Lord to examine us and have Him show us what He sees. This examination by the Lord ensures we are not blinded or deceived in thinking that we are right. We may find that we are right "only in our own eyes." Eternity is too long for us to get this thing wrong. Therefore, we will read on and ask, seek, and knock to ensure we have the connection of sonship with the King of Glory. In the chapter "The Master Plan of Evangelism," we will learn how to share the gospel message properly and effectively with those who are lost and in need of God's saving grace.

> ***Psalms 26:1-2 ESV Of David. Vindicate me, O LORD, for I have walked in my integrity, and I have trusted in the LORD without wavering. (2) Prove me, O LORD, and try me; test my heart and my mind.***

When we examine ourselves and allow the Lord to examine us, we are looking for evidence or proof that we are both "in the faith" and walking "in truth." We can perform the same examinations to evaluate our standing with the Person of the Holy Spirit. There are unmistakable pieces of evidence that the Holy Spirit is walking beside us, wooing us to the heart of the Father and then living within us, making us children of God and a temple of the Holy Spirit. We use this evidence, witnesses, or proof to help evaluate the validity of our faith and our daily Christian walk. There is a great need to examine or assess our Christian life to ensure we are genuinely in the faith, but how do we accomplish this, and what are the pieces of evidence we can trust to evaluate a life-changing event? What measuring tools can we use to examine ourselves and others to ensure that we genuinely possess salvation? Before we experienced the redemption of our soul, before we called on the Name that is above all Names, our Lord Jesus Christ and the Holy Spirit were working on us, wooing us to the heart of the Father. We will start with the three pieces of evidence required before a person is "BORN AGAIN."

Chapter 4
THE THREE SHREDS OF EVIDENCE PROVING THAT THE HOLY SPIRIT IS CONVICTING US

Before our salvation experience, the Holy Spirit walked beside us, wooing our hearts to the Lord Jesus Christ. The Holy Spirit did this by convicting us of three truths, which include sin, righteousness, and judgment.

> *John 16:8-11 ESV And when he comes, he will convict the world concerning sin and righteousness and judgment: (9) concerning sin, because they do not believe in me; (10) concerning righteousness, because I go to the Father, and you will see me no longer; (11) concerning judgment, because the ruler of this world is judged.*

How did we know that we were sinners? It was not because we did things that were wrong or that someone told us. Although these things may give us a mental assent that we may do or think wrong things or make mistakes, we do not realize we are sinners by birth or by nature.

How did we know that Jesus Christ was as righteous as God because He is God? Many people only know Jesus as a baby in the manger we sing about during Christmas. Some may recognize Jesus as the one that died on a cross between two thieves. However, few realize and acknowledge that He is 100% man, but not a mere man, and He is 100% God and was never less than God at any time.

How did we grasp the reality of a place called hell? How did we understand that hell was a place of eternal damnation, punishment, torment, and separation from God the Father? How could we even believe that a loving and forgiving God would allow one of His created beings to go to such a place called hell for eternal judgment? The answers to these questions are found in God's Word, revealed by the Holy Spirit, and annotated in this Book.

It took the Holy Spirit to reveal sin, righteousness, and judgment to us. We had no way of knowing God or the Lord Jesus Christ without the Holy Spirit working in our hearts, revealing truth. It was the Holy Spirit that revealed to us that we were sinners and spiritually lost. Before that convicting revelation, we might have heard that we were sinners but most likely laughed at the notion and believed that we were indeed no better or worse than the next guy. Being a sinner was more than doing immoral things; it was a condition, a status, or a position of the soul before a holy God.

The Holy Spirit convinced and convinced us that Jesus Christ was the Son of God and that He was and is God. We may have heard about a man dying on a cross thousands of years ago, but most likely not phase us at all. Who knows how many Christmas songs we sang and Christmas stories we heard about a new special baby in a manger, without ever considering the ramifications existing because God came down from heaven and wrapped Himself in the flesh of man in order to walk with humanity? Typically, these things are holiday events to get through, yet they carried very little eternal value.

However, that changed for this author on September 4th, 1974, when it became clear who Jesus Christ was and what He had done for us all so that we could experience the salvation of our souls and walk in a relationship with God that Adam enjoyed. The Holy Spirit reveals the judgment of hell and total separation from God without a second chance for repentance. Until that September night, the thought of suffering in hell was a conversational topic in which to joke and mock. It was a curse term we used to express anger towards someone. The thought that it was a place of eternal damnation and separation from God would typically never entertain our thinking process. However, that September night, the Holy Spirit revealed not only the reality of hell but the fact that this young man was headed there for eternity without hope if this heart rejected Jesus Christ as the Son of God and Savior of humanity.

After falling on bended knees and calling out to God for salvation, this author knew that he was forgiven, cleansed, and made a new man. Upon asking the Lord Jesus Christ for forgiveness and accepting this sinner as a son, the Holy Spirit came into this life and took up residence and ownership. When this happens to us, we become children of God and assures us a home in His glory. When the salvation experience is genuine, we know that we know that we have experienced eternal redemption. We typically do not realize it at the time, but soon after true salvation, we manifest all five pieces of evidence or proofs of salvation.

When we experienced redemptive salvation, we called upon the name of our Lord Jesus Christ by faith and believed in our hearts, as spoken of in Romans 10:9-10, 13. We then had the Holy Spirit of the living God dwelling with us.

> ***Romans 10:9-10 ESV because, if you confess with your mouth that Jesus is Lord and believe in your heart that God raised him from the dead, you will be saved. (10) For with the heart one believes and is justified, and with the mouth one confesses and is saved.***

Romans 10:13 ESV For "everyone who calls on the name of the Lord will be saved."

God Himself, the Creator of the universe, chose to dwell within the life of man in the Person of the Holy Spirit.

Romans 8:9 ESV You, however, are not in the flesh but in the Spirit, if in fact the Spirit of God dwells in you. Anyone who does not have the Spirit of Christ does not belong to him.

This revelation is such an incredible reality, knowing that God, His life, His Word, and His righteousness lives within us. This indwelling was made possible because of the cross and our calling upon Jesus to save us. In John 3:8, we find that our Lord Jesus Christ spoke with the Jewish religious teacher Nicodemus and described "true believers" as "everyone who is born of the Spirit." He used the natural act of childbirth, which everyone would know and understand, to describe the spiritual change in anyone responding to the saving work of the Holy Spirit.

John 3:5-9 ESV Jesus answered, "Truly, truly, I say to you, unless one is born of water and the Spirit, he cannot enter the kingdom of God. (6) That which is born of the flesh is flesh, and that which is born of the Spirit is spirit. (7) Do not marvel that I said to you, 'You must be born again.' (8) The wind blows where it wishes, and you hear its sound, but you do not know where it comes from or where it goes. So it is with everyone who is born of the Spirit." (9) Nicodemus said to him, "How can these things be?"

It is God's Holy Spirit that witnesses to our spirit that we are children of God.

Romans 8:15-16 ESV For you did not receive the spirit of slavery to fall back into fear, but you have received the Spirit of adoption as sons, by whom we cry, "Abba! Father!" (16) The Spirit himself bears witness with our spirit that we are children of God,

When we speak about the Holy Spirit dwelling in us, there are many different terms used. We could interchange the word with "dwell with, tabernacles, abides, or lives in us." When we experience genuine salvation, we become the temple of the Holy Spirit. This indwelling of God's Spirit allows us the right to be called sons of God with the promise of individual rights and authority.

John 1:12 ESV But to all who did receive him, who believed in his name, he gave the right to become children of God,

When we called upon the name of the Lord Jesus Christ and believed in our heart, according to Romans 10:9-10, the Holy Spirit of Almighty God moved inside us and made us the temple of the Most-High God. As the temple of the Holy Spirit and the temple of God, we have the same power as our Lord Jesus Christ did when He walked the earth. We have the power of the indwelling Holy Spirit within us that will allow us to operate as our Lord Jesus Christ operated. This truth is why our Lord gave the great promise in John chapter 14 of the things we can do because He sent the Holy Spirit to be within us after He ascended back into heaven.

***John 14:12-14 ESV** "Truly, truly, I say to you, whoever believes in me will also do the works that I do; and greater works than these will he do, because I am going to the Father. (13) Whatever you ask in my name, this I will do, that the Father may be glorified in the Son. (14) If you ask me anything in my name, I will do it.*

Let us revisit the evidence, proof, or assurance that the Holy Spirit is walking beside us, taken from the Scripture of John 16:8-11. The evidence of having the Holy Spirit beside us is that we are convicted or convinced of three things: First, the conviction comes that we are sinners and cannot save ourselves. We are not only sinners from the fact that we sin, but we are sinners by nature. We were born sinners and must be born again to be saints. Secondly, the conviction comes that there is a judgment upon humanity because we are sinners, resulting in total and eternal separation from God and heaven. Thirdly, conviction comes that our Lord Jesus Christ is the Righteous One, the Son of God, and the only One who can save us. He is the Son of God and part of the Godhead, which we call the Trinity, making Jesus Christ God.

Now that we have settled the three pieces of evidence of having the Holy Spirit walking beside us, it is time to get deeper into the salvation process.

There are also pieces of evidence or proof of having the Holy Spirit at work within us. This evidence is called the "five witnesses of salvation." We must have all five of these pieces of evidence as proof of genuine salvation. People may see one of the pieces of evidence in someone, but any of these witnesses or pieces of evidence can be faked by the enemy or faked by the person trying to make us believe they have experienced salvation. None of the five components of evidence can stand alone. Someone who is genuinely "born again, saved, or redeemed" and has the Holy Spirit resident within them will manifest all five of the witnesses, pieces of evidence, proofs, and assurances of true salvation.

This preacher remembers an encounter years ago when witnessing to a young man who was a member of a particular religious faith. In the witnessing process, the questions remained the same, "Are you saved?" "Are you a Christian?" Each time these questions were asked, the response was, "No, I am a..." and would name his religious affiliation. This young man repeatedly was taken back to the Scriptures about receiving the Lord Jesus Christ as Savior as an act of faith for genuine salvation. The explanation that salvation was an act of God's grace and a gift to be received and cannot be earned through the traditions of man or belonging to a particular religious group came forth many times in the witnessing encounter. He agreed to research it further.

The following week there happened to be another encounter with the young man whom this time seemed to overflow with joy. He opened the conversation with the news that he had a salvation experience to share. Even though the young man was heartfelt and joyful, there was a check or hesitancy within my heart. Something was not right. It is not a "judging" thing. Still, we as believers need to remember that we are under no obligation to accept testimonies that are barren of Biblical evidence or Biblical fruit. Even though this young man was saying all the words right, and even though he seemed joyful, something was off.

Therefore, this preacher needed to hear the young man's full testimony from start to finish on how he met the Savior. The young man gleefully recounted his whole religious experience, starting out visiting his first-ever charismatic meeting. According to the young man, when he walked in the door of the church meeting, he felt the Holy Spirit's presence fall on him. He declared that this physical and emotional feeling of the presence of God to be an act of God saving him. Although everything within this heart wanted to believe he had a salvation experience, a Biblical and personal responsibility led this preacher to inform the young man that, according to his testimony, he had not received salvation by faith.

Those who do not trust in Christ by faith are still lost in their sins, no matter their religious experience. I informed and taught the young man that he had experienced the presence of the anointing of God's Holy Spirit, which many people do in their lifetime. Yet, that still does not mean he had experienced the Holy Spirit's indwelling presence as a result of salvation by faith. Let us look at a few Biblical examples. The guards at the tomb of Jesus fell as dead men at the presence of the angels of God, but they still got up unregenerated, not knowing Jesus as Savior. Those armed men who came to arrest Jesus in the garden all fell back on the ground under the power of the Holy Spirit at the spoken words of Jesus. However, they recovered and rose to their feet, tied Him up, and led Him off to trial and crucifixion.

> *John 18:3-6 (ESV) So Judas, having procured a band of soldiers and some officers from the chief priests and the Pharisees, went there with lanterns and torches and weapons. 4 Then Jesus, knowing all that would happen to him, came forward and said to them, "Whom do you seek?" 5 They answered him, "Jesus of Nazareth." Jesus said to them, "I am he." Judas, who betrayed him, was standing with them. 6 When Jesus said to them, "I am he," they drew back and fell to the ground.*

> ***Matthew 28:2-4 (ESV) And behold, there was a great earthquake, for an angel of the Lord descended from heaven and came and rolled back the stone and sat on it. 3 His appearance was like lightning, and his clothing white as snow. 4 And for fear of him the guards trembled and became like dead men.***

Some would say that not believing this young man's testimony is judging, but the fruit always reveals the root. We do not make the Bible align with our experiences or lack of experiences. We must judge, evaluate, and align our experiences with the Word of God and the character of God. We can be passionately and sincerely wrong. It is not about being passionate or sincere about something. It is about doing what the Word of God tells us to do. We experience God's redemptive grace by faith and not by feelings or experiences.

Chapter 5
THE MEASURING TOOL

We live in a world that is ready to believe anything without any proof. A college professor made this statement to one of his students, "Young man, did you know that the two greatest problems in the world today are ignorance and apathy?" The young student looking at the professor answered, "No, sir, I did not know that, and I do not care." This commentary is sad but true among many today. People today are world smart, street smart, media smart, and book smart. In all this temporal worldly intelligence, men have become foolish in their ways and live each day without any established absolutes.

The Bible, the Word of God, has volumes of absolutes based upon concrete proof. The Bible has many claims concerning itself as the witness, evidence, proof, and assurance that it truly is the Word of God. What about the typical professing believer? We all know at least one who professes to know the Lord Jesus Christ, yet if arrested for being a Christian, there would not be any evidence in their lives to convict them.

Millions and millions of people around the world today confess to know the Lord Jesus Christ and call themselves Christians. In fact, over the years, it has become more and more popular for people to call themselves Christian even though they deny the Bible as God's Holy Word and deny the Deity of the Lord Jesus Christ. What is wrong with this picture? How can someone deny the existence of Hell, the reality of the truth of God's Holy Word, the blood atonement, and the Deity of our Lord Jesus

Christ, yet still in good conscience call themselves a Christian?

Key in on some of the "religious" statements used among mass media, music stars, Hollywood stars, and TV talk show hosts. Comments like "our thoughts and prayers go out to so and so," and "May God bless you and may God bless America." These statements carry a sense of care, kindness, and a religious sense of piety. The words committing to prayer and calling out for God's blessings sound morally pious as they seemingly give the impression of someone devoted to religion and a virtuous lifestyle. However, as stated before, the fruit always reveals the root. Our Lord Jesus Christ said that we would know them by their fruit. However, what is that fruit? What is the tool in which we can distinguish between the actual moral and spiritual person who has genuinely experienced God's salvation versus the person who knows the religious language and for a moment falsely appears to be ethical, moral, and spiritual? Anyone can have a moment whereby they can pretend religious devotion or driven by a high standard of moral motivation.

There must be a measuring tool besides believing what is right in our own eyes. There must be something more significant than "if it feels good, do it." The idea of a prayer of "easy believe-ism" cannot be the standard used to test to see if someone has experienced true salvation or not. When we talk about believing, we are not talking about giving mental assent to a historical fact. True salvation is about placing personal trust in the Lord Jesus Christ as the One who gave His life on the cross of Calvary was buried and then rose again from the dead. The word "believe" comes from the Greek word "pisteuo," which means trusting, relying upon, or placing one's weight upon. When a person puts his faith and trust in Jesus Christ alone as his Savior, he enters the status as a child of God and a member of the redeemed. However, how can we measure this to see if our trust was actually placed in Christ?

If we drive our car down the road and the speed limit on that highway is 55 mph, we need a measuring tool to see how fast we are going. That is why each car has a speedometer. With the speedometer, we have a measuring instrument for our driving speed. The same must be true of those who call themselves Christians. There must be some measuring tool within the Scriptures that we can use to judge if someone is truly a believer or not. We are to judge those who say they are of the faith. We are not to judge those who say they are lost.

> ***1 Corinthians 2:14-15 ESV** **The natural person does not accept the things of the Spirit of God, for they are folly to him, and he is not able to understand them because they are spiritually discerned. (15) The spiritual person judges all things, but is himself to be judged by no one.***

> ***1 Corinthians 5:11-13 ESV** **But now I am writing to you not to associate with anyone who bears the name of brother if he is guilty of sexual immorality or greed, or is an idolater, reviler, drunkard, or swindler—not even to eat with such a one. (12) For what have I to do with judging outsiders? Is it not those inside the church whom you are to judge? (13) God judges those outside. "Purge the evil person from among you."***

> ***1 Corinthians 6:2-3 ESV** **Or do you not know that the saints will judge the world? And if the world is to be judged by you, are you incompetent to try trivial cases? (3) Do you not know that we are to judge angels? How much more, then, matters pertaining to this life!***

That is why our Lord said that we would know them by their fruit. Within the Word of God, there are five witnesses, pieces of evidence, proofs, or assurances of how we can know that we are believers and have the Holy Spirit dwelling in us. Some say there are more witnesses or shreds of evidence that a person has experienced salvation. Some have written that there are as many as twelve within the Scriptures, which may be true. However, upon examination, many are just duplications of the five main witnesses or pieces of evidence reworded using different Scriptures. It is the heart of the Father that we know for sure concerning ourselves in salvation and those who labor among us. Having salvation is something that we should know with absolute certainty that we possess because eternity is too long to be wrong.

Not only can we know for sure that we possess true salvation, but we can use the same tools, evidence, and proof on others who claim to have experienced God's redemption. As a Pastor of 40 plus years, it is evident that one of the most significant problems the pastor faces in the church is lost, church members. Years ago, the late Dr. Billy Graham wrote and posted an article whereby he believed that over one-third of the church membership is lost. Religious, yes. Moral, yes. Tithers, yes. Bible readers, yes. Sunday School teachers, yes. However, despite all this, many are spiritually lost, knowing about God but not knowing God. They have a form of religion that knows "about" God, but it is mental assent whereby they failed to mix their confession of mouth with a heart of faith. The problem is that they do not personally "know" God and, for the most part, are deceived about their lack of true salvation. One of the enormous mission fields of our day is within the walls of our churches.

1 John 5:13 ESV** **I write these things to you who believe in the name of the Son of God, that you may know that you have eternal life.

Why is this important? Why is it essential that we can prove our salvation with the Word of God? Because the claim to be a Christian cannot rest on emotion, mental assent, the activity of praying a prayer, or supernatural, unexplainable experiences. We need a Biblical way to discern who is faithful and who are false professors of the faith. We need to know who is true because the Word of God says that in the last days, many false teachers, false prophets, false apostles, and false shepherds will come into the flock to deceive many. They will be wolves in sheep's clothing. They will dress like a Christian, talk like a Christian, do the things that Christians do, carry a Bible, and pray, but their hearts will be far from knowing the Lord.

For this reason, we need to examine ourselves and know that we know who we are in Christ. When we ask ourselves, "Am I a Christian?" We need to be able to shout an emphatic YES, based on the Word of God and the heart of faith within us.

SECTION 2

THE FIVE SHREDS OF EVIDENCE OF SALVATION

Chapter 6
THE FIRST WITNESS:
THE SCRIPTURAL TESTIMONY

The first witness, evidence, or proof that a person has had an authentic salvation experience is their *<u>Scriptural Testimony.</u>* This testimony means that people give a personal testimony that they had a time and place in their lives where they called upon the name of our Lord Jesus Christ to come into their lives and save them. It will be following the Scriptures of Romans 10:9-10, 10:13, and Ephesians 2:8-9. A person does not become a Christian by coming and sitting in a church every week any more than parking a wheelbarrow in a garage will cause it to become a new car.

> ***Romans 10:9-10 ESV** because, if you confess with your mouth that Jesus is Lord and believe in your heart that God raised him from the dead, you will be saved. (10) For with the heart one believes and is justified, and with the mouth one confesses and is saved.*
>
> ***Romans 10:13 ESV** For "everyone who calls on the name of the Lord will be saved."*
>
> ***Ephesians 2:8-9 ESV** For by grace you have been saved through faith. And this is not your own doing; it is the gift of God, (9) not a result of works, so that no one may boast.*

<u>PROBLEM:</u>

Each of the five pieces of evidence or proof carries with it a problem. No one evidence or proof of salvation can stand alone. In other words, just because we quote these Scriptures and pray a "sinner's prayer" does not mean that we have experienced salvation. This lack of assurance does not diminish our need to cry out to God for salvation. However, crying out in prayer does not save us; Jesus saves us by faith, not prayer.

Let us take time to reflect on this last statement so that we are clear about it. Prayers do not save people. It is the Lord Jesus Christ who saves people. It is not just the confessing or calling out that saves us. People all over the world pray many times a day. It is not the action, but the object of the action, mixed with a heart of faith. There must be an act of faith exercised in the heart. The action is prayer. However, the object of our prayer needs to be God, and it requires a heart of faith mixed with the act of prayer. How do we know when we are praying that we have a heart of faith? We will discuss this at great length in this book, but for now, remember the phrase "we will always know the root by the fruit."

> *Hebrews 4:2 ESV For good news came to us just as to them, but the message they heard did not benefit them, because they were not united by faith with those who listened.*
>
> *Hebrews 11:6 (ESV) And without faith it is impossible to please him, for whoever would draw near to God must believe that he exists and that he rewards those who seek him.*

There have been far too many Pastors, Sunday School teachers, Vacation Bible School leaders, and other spiritual leaders rushing, intimidating, pressuring, or manipulating people into praying a prayer and then presenting them before the church as a new brother or sister in the Lord. Unfortunately, within days or weeks, many of those "new converts" are back out in the world doing the same things without any change of heart or mind. Many never enter a church building again, yet they carry a false sense of spiritual security. Salvation must be seen and approached as a work of the Holy Spirit alone. If salvation is to be real, then it must be the Holy Spirit calling and the people responding to that call in a confession mixed with exercised faith of the heart. This tendency to react from emotion is why the "confession of faith" by a person cannot stand alone and needs the other four witnesses or pieces of evidence.

We certainly are not saying that we should not pray with people or introduce people to the Lord Jesus Christ. However, we do need to pray for wisdom and use discernment instead of pressuring someone who wishes to decide for Christ. Allowing the Holy Spirit to woo the heart to the spiritual need of salvation is better than convincing the mind of a necessity.

This author had the privilege of being born and raised in Craigsville, Virginia, a small community about 23 miles from Staunton, which is right in the middle of the beautiful Shenandoah Valley in the Blue Ridge Mountains. As a teenager, one of the barbers most folks used in Craigsville was Harold Wade. Most of the town children, teenagers, and dads went to Mr. Wade for their haircuts. Many of them came home complaining that Mr. Wade took between 30 to 60 minutes to cut each head of hair. The reason Mr. Wade took so long to cut someone's hair was that once he got someone in his barber chair, he would start preaching about their need to be saved. Mr. Wade had them in a position that they could not leave, so it was a captive audience. Mr. Wade would not let his customer out of the barber chair until he finished preaching his salvation message to them. Of course, everyone waiting in line for their haircut heard the good news of Jesus over and over again. Remember, faith comes by hearing and hearing by the Word of God.

Romans 10:17 (ESV) So faith comes from hearing, and hearing through the word of Christ.

That same Mr. Wade, the barber, is now Pastor Harold Wade of Lighthouse Church in Swoope, Virginia. He is the most witnessing person for our Lord Jesus Christ; we could ever hope to meet. At the time of this writing, Mr. Wade is 86 years young, still pastoring, and still will tell anyone, anywhere, and at any time about Jesus. His number one question to ask all he meets is whether they have given their life over to the Lord Jesus Christ as their Savior. Mr. Wade was the third person to witness to this author about the Lord Jesus Christ. In 1971, when hitch-hiking to a bar to party, he stopped and told this foolish young man to climb in his vehicle. Mr. Wade immediately began to share the Lord Jesus Christ with me and how this lost sinner needed Christ to be saved. Of course, all one could think about when spiritually dead was the party waiting just a few miles down the road. Therefore, it was easy refusing his words and plea. This foolish young man still went to the bar and got drunk. However, remembering back, it would be a true testimony to admit that it was a miserable night and a bummer of a party because Mr. Wade had planted the seed of God's Word in the heart. Conviction of sin ruled the evening.

Pastor Wade has prayed with untold thousands and thousands of people the "sinner's prayer." We are talking about a Pastor who has led thousands of people one-on-one in prayer concerning their spiritual standing with the Lord Jesus Christ. Recently Pastor Wade shared his belief in his doing this. He said that he knew not all who prayed with him was serious or exercised the heart of faith, which is necessary for salvation. However, if Mr. Wade prayed with no one, then indeed, 100% of the thousands who crossed his path would have most likely remained lost in their sins. However, if just 50% of those he prayed with were genuine and sincere in their prayer and had a heart of faith, then at least 50% of the thousands would have forgiveness of their sins, miss hell, and gain heaven. Can we take our hat off and honor this man of God and man of faith who has committed his life to see people saved and right with God?

The problem is not the leading of people in prayer to accept Christ. The problem is giving them a false assurance that they have been saved and presenting them as a brother or sister in the Lord to others without additional Biblical evidence. We need to be careful that we do not become the super salesman, "soul-winner." These super salesmen pull confessions out of lost souls with a promise that they will go to heaven based on repeating a little sinner's prayer. These try to take the place of the Holy Spirit in the conviction arena and promise lost people liberty where there is no liberty and forgiveness where there has been no confession of faith. In easy believe-ism, a personal conviction of being a sinner, a conviction of Christ's deity, and the fact that God has already pronounced judgment in which we all have been found guilty are out of the equation in favor of getting false coverts. When operating in mental assent confessions, we can offer a fire escape and give lost people verbal consent to us believing in God and His Word. In other words, we provide them with validation to their false sense of assurance. The Word of God addresses the issue of just believing with the intellect.

> *James 2:19 ESV You believe that God is one; you do well. Even the demons believe—and shudder!*

Of course, we know that the demons do not and cannot repent, nor can they obtain mercy and grace, yet they "believe" the same way a lost person can believe without securing salvation. The "easy prayer" seeks a way to find an easy fire escape that has not come from being under the conviction of the Holy Ghost. This "well-meaning" prayer not mixed with a heart of faith is trying to enter the gate of our Lord's sheepfold by some other means than the door. That would make us a thief, according to our Lord. There is something very wrong with that kind of false conversion. Therefore, by examining the other four pieces of evidence or proof, we can identify "easy believe-ism" as meaningless professions by lost sinners led down a wrong road to a hollow, worthless, repeat-after-me statement.

> *John 10:1-2 (ESV) "Truly, truly, I say to you, he who does not enter the sheepfold by the door but climbs in by another way, that man is a thief and a robber. 2 But he who enters by the door is the shepherd of the sheep.*

> *John 5:24 ESV Truly, truly, I say to you, whoever hears my word and believes him who sent me has eternal life. He does not come into judgment, but has passed from death to life.*

> *Matthew 15:8-9 ESV "'This people honors me with their lips, but their heart is far from me; (9) in vain do they*

worship me, teaching as doctrines the commandments of men.'"

The doctrine of salvation is perhaps the most critical doctrine taught in the Bible. To make a mistake in the doctrine of salvation is to either personally go to hell or lead some other person to hell. The philosophy, mindset, and daily practice of easy believe-ism have mostly overtaken some churches and Pastors, leading thousands down a path of false security. We must be careful that we do not seek a testimonial statement of conversion from a lost person without checking the fruit. Far too many of our churches have become like social clubs that make the requirements to join more important than meeting the Lord Jesus Christ for salvation.

Although mainly the cons of seeking a personal testimony have been stated up to this point, the fact remains that we all need an authentic testimony about our conversion experience. Four other pieces of evidence verify or prove that we are indeed a Christian, but the fact remains that all of the other four rests on the first evidence of having an authentic personal testimony. Praying out or crying out to Jesus for salvation is needed; however, remember that prayer to God must meet a heart of faith.

The other four pieces of evidence will examine that prayer and reveal if it was a prayer of faith or not. Not only do we need a personal testimony of our salvation experience, but we also need to be able to share it quickly at all times and in all places. There are three places in the Book of Acts where Paul's testimony can be read and examined. In Acts 9, 22, and 26, we can read the four key elements of an excellent personal testimony.

Why do we need a personal testimony? Well, first, it is one of the critical pieces of evidence that we have experienced God's salvation for ourselves. Secondly, our testimony carries authority. We were there in that encounter with Christ. No one can say it did not happen. Thirdly, our testimony communicates and relates. It is the first-hand experience telling the lost person that we were not always Christians. We had to come to the crisis of faith in our lives also.

Remember, our testimony is significant, and therefore we should not belittle it because thunder and flashing lights do not fill the storylines like the Apostle Paul's testimony. We should always be prepared and ready to share it no matter where we might find ourselves. We need to keep our testimony short and straightforward, void of churchy words and phrases we take for granted, but people outside the church would not understand. We should keep our testimony on point to the four stages and not chase rabbits or allow questions to detour us. In our testimony, we need to give adequate details without exalting sin or the enemy. We should relive our testimony as we tell it, as if seeing ourselves just receiving Christ. It should be fresh, as if our experience in Christ just happened.

The Four Key Elements of a Personal Salvation Testimony:

1. My life before I met Christ.
2. How I realized my need for Christ
3. How I met Christ
4. How my life has changed since I met Christ

MY TESTIMONY

If not done so, read Paul's testimony in Acts chapters 9:1-22; 22:1-21; and 26:1-26 and then using the four-point outline listed above, let us each type out our testimony of faith. It does not need to be lengthy and should be shared in three to five minutes.

From Paul's Testimony:

1. *<u>My life before I met Christ.</u>*

I, Paul, threatened, persecuted, and murdered the followers of Christ (Acts 9:1, 22:4, 24:19, 26:9-11). I asked the leaders for authority to arrest any who called themselves Christians. (Acts9:2, 22:5, 26:12). I am a Jew, educated by Gamaliel into the strict law of the Jews (Acts 22:3, 26:4-5). I approved the death of Stephen (Acts 22:20).

NOW WRITE THE TESTIMONY OF YOUR LIFE BEFORE CHRIST:

My life before I met Christ: EXAMPLES: Consider your religious or nonreligious background. Did you attend church at any time in your life?

2. *How I realized my need for Christ*

Christ revealed Himself to me. (Acts 9:3-6, 22:6-8, 26:13-15). I became blind at the revelation of Christ (Acts 9:8, 22:11). I fasted for three days (Acts 9:9).

NOW WRITE OUT HOW YOU REALIZED YOU NEEDED CHRIST AND SALVATION:

How I realized I needed Christ. EXAMPLES: Medical, mental, emotional, or relational crisis. Empty feeling-aimless-hopeless. The strong conviction of sin and judgment.

3. *How I met Christ*

What should I do? (Acts 22:10). Ananias came to me and prayed for me (Acts 9:17, 22:14-15). I believed and followed in baptism (Acts 9:18, 22:16).

NOW WRITE OUT HOW YOU MET THE LORD JESUS CHRIST AS YOUR SAVIOR.

How did I meet Jesus Christ? EXAMPLE. Did someone witness to you privately? Was it at a church or revival? Was it in a room alone?

4. *How my life has changed since I met Christ*

Paul stayed with the disciples at Damascus (Acts 9:19, 26:16-20). He started preaching that Jesus Christ is the Son of God (Acts 9:20, 22:16-18). Paul gave his testimony (Acts 22:1, 26:1-2). Paul sent to the Gentiles to preach (Acts 22:21). Paul preached to King Agrippa (Acts 26:6-23). Paul now persecuted for the faith as the Jews sought to kill him (Acts 26:21). Paul puts his trust solely in God (Acts 26:22-23). Paul was accused of losing his mind because of his faith in Christ (Acts 26:24).

NOW WRITE OUT HOW YOUR LIFE HAS CHANGED SINCE BEING SAVED:

How has my life changed since meeting Christ? EXAMPLE. I have peace. No fear of death or hell. Job or marriage better. Since of purpose and hope.

Now that we have discussed *the Scriptural Testimony*, the first evidence or proof of salvation, we will now look at the second evidence or proof of salvation, *The Internal Witness.*

Chapter 7
THE SECOND WITNESS: THE INTERNAL WITNESS

Our Lord Jesus Christ talked about the power of two agreeing and having a witness concerning our faith. Our Lord Jesus Christ said that His Father in heaven was His agreement or witness that He was from heaven.

> *Romans 8:9 ESV You, however, are not in the flesh but in the Spirit, if in fact the Spirit of God dwells in you. Anyone who does not have the Spirit of Christ does not belong to him.*
>
> *Matthew 18:19 ESV Again I say to you, if two of you agree on earth about anything they ask, it will be done for them by my Father in heaven.*
>
> *John 8:17-19 ESV In your Law it is written that the testimony of two people is true. (18) I am the one who bears witness about myself, and the Father who sent me bears witness about me." (19) They said to him therefore, "Where is your Father?" Jesus answered, "You know neither me nor my Father. If you knew me, you would know my Father also."*

Just like our Lord Jesus Christ had the agreement or witness of God the Father, we have a heavenly witness, which is our **_Internal Witness_**. When we receive the gift of God's salvation, the Holy Spirit comes to dwell "within us." We then have His witness within that we are saved and have become a child of God. When we experience true salvation, God gives us a personal internal testimony from the Person of the Holy Spirit that we have become a Christian and that we belong to Him. The Holy Spirit brings us to the place of faith. In doing so, He shows us that we are lost, shows us our need for God, and reveals the Lord Jesus Christ as the only one to satisfy that need.

> ***Romans 8:15-16 ESV For you did not receive the spirit of slavery to fall back into fear, but you have received the Spirit of adoption as sons, by whom we cry, "Abba! Father!" (16) The Spirit himself bears witness with our spirit that we are children of God,***

The Holy Spirit within us bears witness with God the Father, and with our spirit, we have received God's salvation. If we are believers, then the Holy Spirit within each of us should bear witness with one another that we are both saved. If there is no witness between us of the indwelling Holy Spirit, then at least one of us is lost.

> ***Galatians 4:6 ESV And because you are sons, God has sent the Spirit of his Son into our hearts, crying, "Abba! Father!"***

PROBLEM:

Each of the five pieces of evidence or proof carries with it a problem. No one evidence or proof of salvation can stand alone. The prayer must be accompanied by a heart of faith. In other words, just because in the _"Scriptural Witness,"_ we pray a "sinner's prayer" does not mean that we have experienced salvation. Likewise, just because we think we "feel" the witness of God's Spirit regarding the _"Internal Witness"_ does not mean that we have experienced salvation.

This internal witness or evidence cannot stand alone because some people claiming to have received Christ as

Savor may not discern that the Holy Spirit is dwelling in them. Therefore, they cannot determine the internal witness of God's Spirit. On the other hand, they may mistake the world's joy or human zeal as evidence that the Holy Spirit is within them. Some people seeking God may mistake the love and encouragement from fellow Christians as evidence that they have the witness of the Holy Spirit within them.

It is essential to seek the witness of others to see if they sense Christ living in us. It is important not to confuse human zeal and happiness with the indwelling of the person of the Holy Spirit. Again, we need all five pieces of evidence in operation for positive proof of salvation. No one evidence can stand or fall on its own.

1 John 4:13-14 ESV By this we know that we abide in him and he in us, because he has given us of his Spirit. (14) And we have seen and testify that the Father has sent his Son to be the Savior of the world.

Each of us had different experiences when we met the Lord Jesus Christ as our Savior. With some, it was in a church. With others, it may have been at home, the home of a close friend, or outside while experiencing God's beautiful creation. When this writer met Jesus, it was at 01:00 in the morning on September 4, 1974, in a military dorm room. No one had to explain, convince, or assure the fact that the salvation of a soul happened in that room that night. Before September 1974, there had been a few isolated occasions when the conviction of the Holy Spirit had occurred. When that happened, it usually led to the praying of the "sinner's prayer" with a pastor or Sunday School teacher. Each time such an occurrence happened, there was an overwhelming feeling that nothing supernatural had occurred upon walking away, and the promised life change did not take place.

However, that September night in 1974 was radically different. This young man cried out to God for salvation with a heart of faith and desperation. Again, this event happened at 1 am. The Person of the Holy Spirit entered this broken-down drug-filled life and changed it instantly into the tabernacle of the living God. From 01:00-07:00 am, praises rang out in that dorm room while sitting on the edge of the bed and thanking God for His salvation. In total amazement and astonishment, a confession of praise kept flowing forth over and over, "Wow, I am a child of God and truly a Christian."

How was it possible that without a preacher, a teacher, or having a Bible to read, could such assurance exist? The answer was the indwelling Holy Spirit. The internal witness of the Holy Spirit bore witness with the soulish man that God had answered the prayer of faith and that genuine salvation took place. The prayer of faith is far more than just a prayer; it is an eternal life-changing event. As we said before, no single evidence of salvation can stand alone. We need to have both the ***Scriptural Testimony*** and an ***Internal Witness*** from the Holy Spirit as evidence of true salvation.

Chapter 8
THE THIRD WITNESS:
THE EXTERNAL WITNESS:

Now that we have discussed the *Scriptural Testimony* and the *Internal Witness*, we will look at the third evidence of salvation, the *External Witness*. What evidence in the way of an external witness of the Holy Spirit's indwelling do we think could be seen by others? Two primary pieces of evidence can be witnessed by others: a changed life and the fruit of the Spirit.

These two go hand in hand. One cannot manifest the fruit of the Holy Spirit without having a changed lifestyle. The fruit of the Spirit is also the character of God or who He is. The Apostle Paul lists the fruit of the Holy Spirit in Gal.5:22-23, which includes *Love, Joy, Peace, Patience, Kindness, Goodness, Faithfulness, Gentleness, and Self-Control*. Remember that our heavenly Father does each of these nine fruits as an action of His character, but they are more than acts of God towards us. These nine fruits are who God is or that which makes up His character. God loves as a choice and action, but God is love as His character. We need to wrap our mind around the fact that each of these is God's character traits, which He deposited within us by way of the indwelling Holy Spirit at the moment of salvation.

Trying to live a Christian life can be very frustrating at times. Guess what? We do not have to try to live the Christian life. In fact, we cannot live the Christian life. It takes God to live His life in and through us, which is the only way to experience a victorious Christian life. The Person of the Holy Spirit helps us live the Christian life in reality and substance by living God's life through us. We cannot come to God on our own. The Holy Spirit woos our heart to the Father. Once we experience God's wonderful gift of salvation, the Holy Spirit comes within us to set up residence and ownership. When He comes within us, He establishes in our spirit-man the character of God known as the fruit of the Spirit. As we grow in the Lord, the fruit of the Holy Spirit (the character of God) is manifested in our soulish man and our physical man so *others might see God in us*.

A phrase used often in this book is, **"The fruit always reveals the root"** applies here. People who are spiritually lost can never bear the fruit of the Holy Spirit or the character and nature of God. However, people spiritually redeemed must bear the fruit of the Holy Spirit or the character and nature of God because this fruit is one of the pieces of evidence of salvation. One of the false catchphrases heard inside and outside of the church is that we are ALL God's children. We are all God's creation, but we are NOT ALL God's children. We must be genuinely born again by the Holy Spirit to be adopted into the family of God and become one of His children. Moreover, with that new birth comes the impartation of God's character as proof of sonship.

> *Galatians 5:22-25 ESV But the fruit of the Spirit is love, joy, peace, patience, kindness, goodness, faithfulness, (23) gentleness, self-control; against such things there is no law. (24) And those who belong to Christ Jesus have crucified the flesh with its passions and desires. (25) If we live by the Spirit, let us also keep in step with the Spirit.*

2 Corinthians 5:17 ESV Therefore, if anyone is in Christ, he is a new creation. The old has passed away; behold, the new has come.

John 1:12-13 ESV But to all who did receive him, who believed in his name, he gave the right to become children of God, (13) who were born, not of blood nor of the will of the flesh nor of the will of man, but of God.

When people give or surrender their lives to the Lord Jesus Christ and are truly born again, they are not the same, and the manifestation of the fruit of the Holy Spirit reveals it. As stated before, the fruit of the Holy Spirit is not just what God does; it is who God is. God does more than love us in action. God is love. How important is it to see the fruit of the Holy Spirit in a person's life? Because the fruit reveals the root. If there is no fruit of the Holy Spirit, then that person is not connected to the Lord Jesus Christ.

Matthew 7:16-20 ESV You will recognize them by their fruits. Are grapes gathered from thornbushes, or figs from thistles? (17) So, every healthy tree bears good fruit, but the diseased tree bears bad fruit. (18) A healthy tree cannot bear bad fruit, nor can a diseased tree bear good fruit. (19) Every tree that does not bear good fruit is cut down and thrown into the fire. (20) Thus you will recognize them by their fruits.

There are two great teachers of God's Word. The first being the most important, which is the Person of the Holy Spirit. The Bible says that He will guide us into all truth. The second teacher is repetition. Experts have studied the aspect of hearing in almost every possible field and vocation. We are not speaking about physical hearing but mental and emotional hearing. The conclusion is that a person does not "hear" something until hearing it for the seventh time. Also, it is interesting that a person needs to hear that same truth twenty-one times before it starts making an impact or change in their life and daily thinking and habits.

> ***John 16:13 (ESV) When the Spirit of truth comes, he will guide you into all the truth, for he will not speak on his own authority, but whatever he hears he will speak, and he will declare to you the things that are to come.***
>
> ***Luke 12:12 (ESV) for the Holy Spirit will teach you in that very hour what you ought to say."***
>
> ***John 14:26 (ESV) But the Helper, the Holy Spirit, whom the Father will send in my name, he will teach you all things and bring to your remembrance all that I have said to you.***

Now to the repetition side of teaching. When people have genuinely experienced salvation, they must manifest the fruit of the Spirit. This fruit is the external witness or evidence which others can see. It is the character of God lived out through us. Why all of the fuss about repeating this, we might ask? After over 40 years of ministry, it is a sad commentary to state that some of the meanest, most disrespectful, and rebellious people anyone would want to deal with unfortunately represent the Christian faith and fill the pews of our churches. Yes, they have a testimony of praying a prayer sometime back in their past. Yes, they followed the commands of baptism, joined and attended church, read their Bibles, gave their tithes, and many times taught Sunday School classes, yet the evidence of the fruit of the Holy Spirit has never manifested in and through their lives.

Our Lord Jesus Christ said that we would know them by their fruit and not by their church presence, physical or spiritual gifts, or their testimony. Our Lord said, "they tell me that they love me with their lips, but their heart is far from me."

> *Matthew 12:33 ESV "Either make the tree good and its fruit good, or make the tree bad and its fruit bad, for the tree is known by its fruit.*
>
> *Matthew 15:8-9 (ESV) "'This people honors me with their lips, but their heart is far from me; 9 in vain do they worship me, teaching as doctrines the commandments of men.'"*

Reading the Bible, going to the church, tithing, praying, and other disciplines of the faith are all essential mandates of the Christian life. However, they certainly do not qualify as the fruit of the Holy Spirit and are not pieces of evidence, proofs, and witnesses of salvation. Although we should do these things because they are spiritual disciplines listed within the Word of God, understand that lost religious people could do many of these disciplines without knowing the truth.

> *Luke 6:32-34 ESV "If you love those who love you, what benefit is that to you? For even sinners love those who love them. (33) And if you do good to those who do good to you, what benefit is that to you? For even sinners do the same. (34) And if you lend to those from whom you expect to receive, what credit is that to you? Even sinners lend to sinners, to get back the same amount.*

Luke 6:43-45 ESV "For no good tree bears bad fruit, nor again does a bad tree bear good fruit, (44) for each tree is known by its own fruit. For figs are not gathered from thornbushes, nor are grapes picked from a bramble bush. (45) The good person out of the good treasure of his heart produces good, and the evil person out of his evil treasure produces evil, for out of the abundance of the heart his mouth speaks.

Matthew 15:8-9 ESV "'This people honors me with their lips, but their heart is far from me; (9) in vain do they worship me, teaching as doctrines the commandments of men.'"

2 Timothy 3:6-8 ESV For among them are those who creep into households and capture weak women, burdened with sins and led astray by various passions, (7) always learning and never able to arrive at a knowledge of the truth. (8) Just as Jannes and Jambres opposed Moses, so these men also oppose the truth, men corrupted in mind and disqualified regarding the faith.

We need to keep in mind that the fruit of the Holy Spirit is different from the signs and wonders of the Holy Spirit. Those who do signs and wonders are not manifesting evidence that they have experienced God's gift of salvation. The Scriptures state that many believers will be deceived in the end-times as wolves in sheep clothing come and perform great signs and wonders. We also have testimony from our Lord Jesus Christ of a religious leader who performed signs and wonders, yet our Lord said that He never knew the man. This statement from our Lord reveals that this religious leader was lost and performed extraordinary things using our Lord's name but never knowing Him as Lord and

Savior. Our Lord Jesus Christ called the man's works (his signs and wonders) as works of iniquity. This end-time deception is why our Lord stated that we would know them by their fruit and not by their signs.

> *Matthew 24:24 ESV For false christs and false prophets will arise and perform great signs and wonders, so as to lead astray, if possible, even the elect.*
>
> *Mark 13:22 ESV For false christs and false prophets will arise and perform signs and wonders, to lead astray, if possible, the elect.*
>
> *2 Thessalonians 2:9-12 ESV The coming of the lawless one is by the activity of Satan with all power and false signs and wonders, (10) and with all wicked deception for those who are perishing, because they refused to love the truth and so be saved. (11) Therefore God sends them a strong delusion, so that they may believe what is false, (12) in order that all may be condemned who did not believe the truth but had pleasure in unrighteousness.*
>
> *Matthew 7:21-23 ESV "Not everyone who says to me, 'Lord, Lord,' will enter the kingdom of heaven, but the one who does the will of my Father who is in heaven. (22) On that day many will say to me, 'Lord, Lord, did we not prophesy in your name, and cast out demons in your name, and do many mighty works in your name?' (23) And then will I declare to them, 'I never knew you; depart from me, you workers of lawlessness.'*

PROBLEM:

Each of the five pieces of evidence or proofs carries with it a problem. No one evidence or proof of salvation can stand alone. In other words, just because in the <u>*"Scriptural*</u>

Witness," we pray a "sinner's prayer" does not mean that we have experienced salvation. Just because we think we "feel" the witness of God's Spirit regarding the ***"Internal Witness"*** does not mean that we have experienced salvation. And just because we see traits of the fruit of the Holy Spirit such as *Love, Joy, Peace, Patience, Kindness, Goodness, Faithfulness, Gentleness, and Self-Control* does not mean that we experienced salvation or manifesting the ***External Witness.***

This witness or evidence of the fruit of the Holy Spirit cannot stand alone because people can become more moral by hanging around other moral people. Also, for each fruit listed in Gal.5:22-23 that is of the Holy Spirit, a fleshly substitute can mimic the real thing. Take the first fruit of the Holy Spirit on the list, which is love. This word is "agape" and represents God's unconditional love, kindness, and mercy. God gives what we do not deserve and cannot earn just because of the Father's love. In the natural, we have four other words for love that are fleshly and conditional.

1. Phileo or friendship love.
2. Eros or romantic love.
3. Epithumia or overly desiring, craving, longing such as lust.
4. Storge, or "old shoe" love, is a love between a couple where they are comfortable with one another. Familiar love.

The problem is that none of these four loves can give wholly and unconditionally. The same is true with the false fleshly substitute for each of the nine fruit of Galatians 5:22-25. Some people choose to walk in such a way that their morals change for the better. If not careful, we can look at these moral changes and assume they have had a spiritual change by encountering the Holy Spirit. God, however, has not called us to morality. He has called us to His righteousness. We can become more moral in our thinking and behavior, better in our social relationships and personal habits without ever having the righteousness of God and experiencing salvation.

Remember that there were two trees in the garden of Eden. There was the tree of life and the tree of the knowledge of good and evil. The good on the tree of "knowledge of good and evil" is just as bad as the evil is. Why? Because God did not call us to be moral, He has called us to be righteous. Becoming righteous only happens when we eat from the tree of life (Jesus). When someone is lost and wants to be a part of the church like it is a social club, it becomes easy to change morals to that which is acceptable among the group. However, this moral change is not walking in the fruit of the Holy Spirit, nor is it evidence of salvation.

> *1 John 3:7-10 ESV Little children, let no one deceive you. Whoever practices righteousness is righteous, as he is righteous. (8) Whoever makes a practice of sinning is of the devil, for the devil has been sinning from the beginning. The reason the Son of God appeared was to destroy the works of the devil. (9) No one born of God makes a practice of sinning, for God's seed abides in him; and he cannot keep on sinning, because he has been born of God. (10) By this it is evident who are the children of God, and who are the children of the devil: whoever does not practice righteousness is not of God, nor is the one who does not love his brother.*

A true believer, who has the righteousness of God because of true salvation, will become more moral in their practical life in word, deed, and thought. Morality has no absolutes and varies from culture to culture, family to family, and person to person. Morality is believing and doing what we feel is right in our own eyes, which the Scriptures warns us about repeatedly. We can have a level of morality without being righteous, but as we choose to walk in the righteousness of God, we will be more moral. Personal, social, or cultural morality without God's righteousness has only one absolute, and that is, "There are no absolutes."

Therefore, everyone does what is right in their own eyes and establishes their level of morality. God's righteousness, however, is absolute and is, in every way, "unchangeable." Based on His character and His Word, God's righteousness stands true because of His immutability. God cannot change or fail.

First, we will look at some Scriptures about being right in one's own eyes. Second, we will examine the Scriptures about being right in the eyes of the Lord. Third, we will look at the Scriptures declaring the immutability of God.

Doing what is right in our own eyes: Our Morality

> *Numbers 15:39-40 (ESV) And it shall be a tassel for you to look at and remember all the commandments of the LORD, to do them, not to follow after your own heart and your own eyes, which you are inclined to whore after. 40 So you shall remember and do all my commandments, and be holy to your God.*

> *Deuteronomy 12:8 (ESV) "You shall not do according to all that we are doing here today, everyone doing whatever is right in his own eyes,*
>
> *Judges 17:6 (ESV) In those days there was no king in Israel. Everyone did what was right in his own eyes.*
>
> *Proverbs 21:2 (ESV) Every way of a man is right in his own eyes, but the LORD weighs the heart.*
>
> *Proverbs 12:15 (ESV) The way of a fool is right in his own eyes, but a wise man listens to advice.*

Doing what is right in the eyes of the Lord: His righteousness

> *Exodus 15:26 (ESV) saying, "If you will diligently listen to the voice of the LORD your God, and do that which is right in his eyes, and give ear to his commandments and keep all his statutes, I will put none of the diseases on you that I put on the Egyptians, for I am the LORD, your healer."*
>
> *1 Kings 15:4-5 (ESV) Nevertheless, for David's sake the LORD his God gave him a lamp in Jerusalem, setting up his son after him, and establishing Jerusalem, 5 because David did what was right in the eyes of the LORD and did not turn aside from anything that he commanded him all the days of his life, except in the matter of Uriah the Hittite.*

The immutability of God: He is unchanging

> *Hebrews 6:17-18 (ESV) So when God desired to show more convincingly to the heirs of the promise the unchangeable character of his purpose, he guaranteed it*

with an oath, 18 so that by two unchangeable things, in which it is impossible for God to lie, we who have fled for refuge might have strong encouragement to hold fast to the hope set before us.

What about those who are not born again, nor possess the indwelling Holy Spirit, yet incredibly moral and religious? They may come to church each week, pray, and read their Bibles. They may look like Christians, dress like Christians, talk like Christians, and smell like Christians, but the Holy Spirit is not in them. What fruit can we see from those who are void of the Holy Spirit but actively embrace religion, tradition, and religious habits? The fruit will be self-centeredness, sensuality, and blindness towards the truth of God's Word. They will talk about religion, their denomination, work, and activities within the church, but they are uncomfortable speaking about the Lord Jesus Christ. Those who grow up in the church scene can develop the habits of church life from their Christian parents or friends, yet still be lost and without the indwelling Holy Spirit. Those in the church who do not have the indwelling of the Holy Spirit are sensual, according to Jude 1:17-19.

Jude 1:17-19 ESV But you must remember, beloved, the predictions of the apostles of our Lord Jesus Christ. (18) They said to you, "In the last time there will be scoffers, following their own ungodly passions." (19) It is these who cause divisions, worldly people, devoid of the Spirit.

According to Romans 8:9, those in the church who do not have the indwelling Holy Spirit are also without the Lord Jesus Christ.

Romans 8:9 ESV You, however, are not in the flesh but in the Spirit, if in fact the Spirit of God dwells in you. Anyone who does not have the Spirit of Christ does not belong to him.

As we said before, no single evidence of salvation can stand alone. We need to have the **_Scriptural Testimony_** of personal testimony, the **_Internal Witness_** from the Holy Spirit, and the **_External Witness_** of the fruit of the Holy Spirit as evidence of true salvation. Now we will look at the fourth evidence of true salvation, the **_Fraternal Witness._**

Chapter 9
THE FOURTH WITNESS: THE FRATERNAL WITNESS

Now that we have discussed the *Scriptural Testimony*, the *Internal Witness*, and the *External Witness*, we will look at the fourth evidence of salvation, the *Fraternal Witness*. What possible evidence in a fraternal witness do we think could be seen by others? One significant piece of evidence that the world and the church need to see is our love for our Christian brothers.

Spiritual adoption is a great thing. It means that we once belonged to a dysfunctional, judged, and condemned family until we were removed by faith and placed into a great family. Through the work of our Lord Jesus Christ on the cross in redeeming humanity and the wooing of the Holy Spirit to salvation, we can experience the adoption of God. According to the Word of God, when we were lost, our spiritual father was Satan. This fatherhood of Satan is a hard truth, but the truth, nevertheless. When we asked the Lord Jesus Christ to save us, the Holy Spirit came within us, and He made us "children of God." The term "born again" speaks about our spirit-man coming to life and our adoption into the family of God. Once saved, every true believer in the world became our adopted brothers and sisters.

> *Galatians 4:4-5 ESV But when the fullness of time had come, God sent forth his Son, born of woman, born under the law, (5) to redeem those who were under the law, so that we might receive adoption as sons.*

> *John 8:38-44 (ESV) I speak of what I have seen with my Father, and you do what you have heard from your father." 39 They answered him, "Abraham is our father." Jesus said to them, "If you were Abraham's children, you would be doing the works Abraham did, 40 but now you seek to kill me, a man who has told you the truth that I heard from God. This is not what Abraham did. 41 You are doing the works your father did." They said to him, "We were not born of sexual immorality. We have one Father—even God." 42 Jesus said to them, "If God were your Father, you would love me, for I came from God and I am here. I came not of my own accord, but he sent me. 43 Why do you not understand what I say? It is because you cannot bear to hear my word. 44 You are of your father the devil, and your will is to do your father's desires. He was a murderer from the beginning, and does not stand in the truth, because there is no truth in him. When he lies, he speaks out of his own character, for he is a liar and the father of lies.*

The Bible states that before we accepted the Lord Jesus Christ as Savior, we were sons of the devil. Imagine that; all lost people have the evil one as their father. When we received the Lord Jesus Christ as our Savior, God removed us from that dysfunctional, judged, and condemned family and placed us within His family of forgiven saints. Not only were we put into the family of God, but we became heirs to all the riches of heaven.

> *Romans 8:15-17 ESV For you did not receive the spirit of slavery to fall back into fear, but you have received the Spirit of adoption as sons, by whom we cry, "Abba! Father!" (16) The Spirit himself bears witness with our spirit that we are children of God, (17) and if children,*

then heirs—heirs of God and fellow heirs with Christ, provided we suffer with him in order that we may also be glorified with him.

Therefore, we are spiritual brothers and sisters to all the believers in the world. The Spirit of adoption should cause we have the fraternal evidence of agape love for the brothers and sisters in the Lord. There is no excuse for the lack of love among one another in the body of Christ, except for us possessing false salvation. The Word of God states this clearly. This love for the brothers is a strong defining witness or evidence that we are truly saved and have the indwelling of the Holy Spirit. If we do not love the Christian brothers, we have the proof or evidence that we are deceptive, still lost in our sins, and do not know God. Religious? Yes. Are they committed to a religious system of structure such as a denomination? Yes. However, possessing Biblical salvation? Not according to God's Word.

John 13:35 ESV By this all people will know that you are my disciples, if you have love for one another."

1 John 2:9-11 ESV Whoever says he is in the light and hates his brother is still in darkness. (10) Whoever loves his brother abides in the light, and in him there is no cause for stumbling. (11) But whoever hates his brother is in the darkness and walks in the darkness, and does not know where he is going, because the darkness has blinded his eyes.

1 John 4:20-21 ESV If anyone says, "I love God," and hates his brother, he is a liar; for he who does not love his brother whom he has seen cannot love God whom he has not seen. (21) And this commandment we have from him: whoever loves God must also love his brother.

PROBLEM:
Each of the five pieces of evidence or proofs carries with it a problem. No one evidence or proof of salvation can stand alone. In other words, just because in the ***"Scriptural Witness,"*** we pray a "sinner's prayer" does not mean that we have experienced salvation. Just because we think we "feel" the witness of God's Spirit regarding the ***"Internal Witness"*** does not mean that we have experienced salvation. Just because we see traits of the fruit of the Holy Spirit in our life regarding the ***External Witness*** does not tell that we have experienced salvation. Just because we say that we love one another as Christian brothers and sisters or occasionally show traits of love towards one another does not mean that we have experienced salvation or manifesting the ***Fraternal Witness***.

One of the greatest needs of humanity is the need to belong. People are looking to be accepted and loved. When the world's lost people look at Christians, they are not looking at their Bible knowledge, ability to pray, or knowledge to quote Scriptures. The world is looking at the Christian's command to love one another and love them.

It should shock and amaze us that lost people can enter a bar, sit down on a barstool next to a stranger, and in five minutes, they are sharing life stories and laughing like they are life-long friends. However, those who profess Christ, supposed to love one another and walk in forgiveness, can come into church on Sunday morning and walk out of their way to keep from greeting one another. Let us be honest for a moment. How much do we know about the Christian brothers and sisters where we attend church? How much do they know about us? Why are we so emotionally closed with the ones God commands us to love and fellowship with and with those we are to receive God's love? This attitude is not the love of God the Bible reveals and our Lord displayed.

Back in 1974, before receiving the Lord's salvation, this writer was filled with anger, hatred, racism, and unforgiveness. After experiencing redemption that September 4th night, no one had to teach that we needed to love one another, forgive one another, and attend fellowship with one another. The Holy Spirit's supernatural work within us changed us and revealed salvation by our genuine love for the brothers. It would be easy for us to say that we love all the people in China because it costs us nothing when we do not know them and do not have daily contact. It would be noncommittal words that carried no strings of action or cost. However, how can we say that we are Christians and stay out of all fellowship contact with the Christian brothers and sisters around us? The Word of God commands us to fellowship with one another. We cannot do that sitting home isolated from the gathering of saints with excuses as to why we do not need to participate.

> *1 John 4:7-8 ESV Beloved, let us love one another, for love is from God, and whoever loves has been born of God and knows God. (8) Anyone who does not love does not know God, because God is love.*

> *Hebrews 10:24-25 ESV And let us consider how to stir up one another to love and good works, (25) not neglecting to meet together, as is the habit of some, but encouraging one another, and all the more as you see the Day drawing near.*

The need to be loved and accepted are strong emotions among humanity. We all have seen lost people come into the church, and because of the acceptance and love they felt, they began to "fit" in the group. They had their need to belong fulfilled even though they had not been born again. We are to show God's love to the lost among us. However, we should not treat them as though they are Christian brothers and sisters. If we genuinely love them, we will tell them the complete gospel message of their need to be saved, even if it offends them.

As we said before, no single evidence of salvation can stand alone. We need to have the ***Scriptural Testimony*** of personal testimony, the ***Internal Witness*** from the Holy Spirit, the ***External Witness*** of the fruit of the Holy Spirit, and the ***Fraternal Witness*** by loving our Christian brothers as evidence of true salvation. Now we will look at the fifth evidence of true salvation, which is the ***Paternal Witness***.

Chapter 10
THE FIFTH WITNESS: THE PATERNAL WITNESS

Now that we have discussed the *__Scriptural Testimony__*, the *__Internal Witness__*, the *__External Witness__*, and the *__Fraternal Witness__*, we will look at the fifth evidence of salvation, the *__Paternal Witness__*. What possible evidence in a paternal witness do we think could be seen by others? One significant piece of evidence that we see lacking in the church is having the Father's discipline when we are in sin.

The fifth and final witness or evidence that we have experienced genuine salvation, and the Holy Spirit is within us is the paternal witness. This evidence is the manifestation of the Fatherhood of God, whereby He loves us through chastening us when we are out of fellowship or walking in sin. This work of the Father is certainly not one of our favorite pieces of evidence revealing our true salvation, but undoubtedly significant.

Most of us can remember as a child when our parents would discipline us when we were disobedient or rebellious. That disciple may have come in many different methods and served in varying degrees. Sometimes it was just what we needed for the disobedience we committed, and sometimes, unfortunately, it was overly extreme and close to abusive. Sometimes it was given from a loving and affectionate heart, and sometimes it was administered out of anger, frustration, and lack of self-control.

We are about to touch on an emotional issue. However, let us remember that any argument must be directed to God because it is His written Word and ***NOT*** how we feel or think about the topic. Back growing up in the mountains of Virginia, the discipline we received in our family among our siblings was not a timeout or a "count to five" to make us stop our undesirable behavior.

Our dad was not a Christian in his early days, yet he believed in the Scriptural advice about not sparing the rod. In today's society and with the current laws of the land, our dad would most likely face accusations for child abuse for some of the spanking we received. It would have been more likely than not that we would have been removed from our home and placed in a foster home. It is not that we felt or thought that we suffered from physical abuse because we believed all children experienced spanking with a switch, a belt, or a paddle as a means of discipline. In defense of our dad, though, he did not discipline us out of anger but out of love. The discipline, though severe and unpleasant, worked towards our knowing right from wrong. Furthermore, we never received a punishment we did not deserve.

We can readily look at society today and see the fruit of our laws concerning raising children and see that the current measures of discipline are not working. Could this lack of discipline today be one of the contributing factors of children going on killing sprees? We are not trying to be political or tell people how to raise their children, but many of us talk about the good old days. Many of us can remember the days when life was simpler and safer. Our house doors did not have locks; families ate their meals together and shared entertainment around the TV. Some of the biggest problems our teenagers got into trouble over in school were chewing gum in class, running in the halls, and racing their cars out of the school parking lots. We did not fear drive-by shootings, kids killings kids in our schools, and bomb threats.

We need to step back and be honest about why our children and youth are more rebellious towards parents and authority, less respectful towards adults and themselves, and possess total disregard for law and order. Has our fear of going overboard with discipline resulted in us throwing the baby out with the bathwater, per se?

If we have a problem with disciplining children, we might have a problem with the fifth evidence that someone is genuinely born again. The fifth evidence of possessing an authentic salvation experience is that God chastens, disciplines, and spanks us because we are His children, and He is our Father. He does not chasten, discipline, or spank illegitimate children (those who are not His).

The Father teaches us that we desire the same example for our children as He spanks or disciplines us. He tells us that He spanks or disciplines us because He loves us, and we should show the same love to our children. Now that some of us are most likely upset or bothered by this let us look at the Word of God and see what the Father tells us. First, remember one of this author's quotable quotes about Christians and the Word of God. "Christians will believe everything you teach, as long as you teach what they already believe."

> *Proverbs 13:24 ESV Whoever spares the rod hates his son, but he who loves him is diligent to discipline him.*

The word "betimes" in the KJV and "diligent" in the ESV is "Shachar" and means to chasten early.

> *Proverbs 22:15 ESV Folly is bound up in the heart of a child, but the rod of discipline drives it far from him.*

Proverbs 29:15 ESV The rod and reproof give wisdom, but a child left to himself brings shame to his mother.

As a child of God with the indwelling of the Holy Spirit, we must have the paternal witness or evidence of our heavenly Father. The witness or evidence of the Father is His chastening of us when we are disobedient. He blesses us when we are obedient; however, He also disciplines or spanks us when we are disobedient. The Father only chastens His children and does not chasten the children of the enemy. If we are wrong and living in sin, and the Father is not dealing with us concerning this sin, then we are not manifesting one of the pieces of evidence of true Biblical salvation.

One could almost hear someone screaming right now, "This is judging. I know that I have experienced salvation." We should not argue from emotion or from what we want to believe. Let the Word of God be true and stand for itself. Remember that the Word is Christ, and Christ is the Word. To reject the Word is to reject Christ.

John 1:1 (ESV) In the beginning was the Word, and the Word was with God, and the Word was God.

John 1:14 (ESV) And the Word became flesh and dwelt among us, and we have seen his glory, glory as of the only Son from the Father, full of grace and truth.

Revelation 19:13 (ESV) He is clothed in a robe dipped in blood, and the name by which he is called is The Word of God.

It must be communicated that God does not discipline or chasten His children out of anger, frustration, desperation, or hurt. God is not like our earthly fathers. However, our earthly fathers are supposed to be like God. God is perfect in His ways and actions. He never goes overboard in His actions, and He is never out of control emotionally. He knows what we need and when we need it to get us to come back to a place of righteousness and walking in the light as He is in the light. God does not provoke us to anger. All the disciplining He does is to produce the fruit of righteousness in us.

> *Hebrews 12:5-11 ESV And have you forgotten the exhortation that addresses you as sons? "My son, do not regard lightly the discipline of the Lord, nor be weary when reproved by him. (6) For the Lord disciplines the one he loves, and chastises every son whom he receives." (7) It is for discipline that you have to endure. God is treating you as sons. For what son is there whom his father does not discipline? (8) If you are left without discipline, in which all have participated, then you are illegitimate children and not sons. (9) Besides this, we have had earthly fathers who disciplined us and we respected them. Shall we not much more be subject to the Father of spirits and live? (10) For they disciplined us for a short time as it seemed best to them, but he disciplines us for our good, that we may share his holiness. (11) For the moment all discipline seems painful rather than pleasant, but later it yields the peaceful fruit of righteousness to those who have been trained by it.*

PROBLEM:

Each of the five pieces of evidence or proofs carries with it a problem. No one evidence or proof of salvation can stand alone. In other words, just because in the **_Scriptural Witness,_** we pray a "sinner's prayer" does not mean that we have experienced salvation. Just because we think we "feel" the witness of God's Spirit regarding the *Internal Witness* does not mean that we have experienced salvation. Just because we see traits of the fruit of the Holy Spirit in our life regarding the *External Witness* does not tell that we have experienced salvation. Just because we love one another as Christian brothers and sisters regarding the *Fraternal Witness* does not mean we have experienced salvation. Likewise, just because we seem to be receiving trials and tribulations, which may resemble God's chastisement, does not mean that we have experienced salvation or manifesting the *Paternal Witness*.

Every person on the earth has troubles, trials, and temptations. Many of these troubles are brought on by reaping what we have sown or by making bad decisions. It is challenging to know the difference between God chastening His children versus the world and the enemy beating up people emotionally, mentally, financially, or relationally.

We can tell the difference by looking at the fruit or character trait the problem or trial produces. The Father releases His chastening hands on us to bring about in our lives the peaceable fruit of righteousness. It will always be for our good, even though the Scriptures say that it is severe, and at the time, we cannot see any good in it.

The fruit the enemy wants to bring about is blame, bitterness, faithlessness, and unforgiveness. We need to remember that the Scriptures clearly state that the heavenly Father cannot tempt us, nor can He be tempted. Some would blame God for a temptation that caused them to sin. Temptation comes from lust in our hearts or the enemy, Satan and the demons, but never from God.

***James 1:13-15 ESV** **Let no one say when he is tempted, "I am being tempted by God," for God cannot be tempted with evil, and he himself tempts no one. (14) But each person is tempted when he is lured and enticed by his own desire. (15) Then desire when it has conceived gives birth to sin, and sin when it is fully grown brings forth death.*

True salvation will carry Biblical evidence. We shall know those who call themselves Christians by their fruit. We need a _**scriptural testimony**_, an _**internal witness**_, an _**external witness**_, a _**fraternal witness**_, and a _**paternal witness**_ as evidence of true salvation. We must bear all five as evidence of genuine salvation. The Apostle Paul says that we need to examine ourselves. Now we have the measuring tool, which is God's standard whereby we have the right to call ourselves "children of God." May we be found faithful and true.

SECTION 3

THE FRUIT OF THE HOLY SPIRIT

Chapter 11
THE FRUIT OF THE HOLY SPIRIT

Many in the body of Christ have heard teaching concerning the fruit of the Spirit and may have wondered what it is precisely and how it relates to us being Christian. In Galatians 5:22-23, the Apostle Paul gives us a list of nine characteristics of God called "the fruit of the Spirit.

Galatians 5:22-23 (ESV) But the fruit of the Spirit is love, joy, peace, patience, kindness, goodness, faithfulness, 23 gentleness, self-control; against such things there is no law.

1. Love
2. Joy
3. Peace
4. Forbearance (Patience)
5. Kindness
6. Goodness
7. Faithfulness
8. Gentleness
9. Self-control

These nine "fruit" or characteristics result from the Holy Spirit's work in a Christian's life and are one of five pieces of evidence that a person is genuinely born again. People who are spiritually lost cannot manifest the fruit of the Spirit; however, all and genuine believers must do so.

The Greek word translated "fruit" usually refers to the natural product of a living thing, in the sense of something edible like fruits and vegetables. However, we can also translate "fruit" as offspring, a deed, action, result, or profit. We might even use the word "fruit" as the "fruit of our labor" to communicate the results of our hard work or a finished project.

In Galatians 5:22-23, the word "fruit" can mean a deed, action, or result. The Holy Spirit guided Paul to use the term "fruit" to help us understand the product of the work and ministry of the Holy Spirit within each believer. This definition should help us realize how personal this ministry and work of the Holy Spirit are within us. We are to be Christ-like, but how is that to happen, and what does it look like?

The fruit of the Spirit is a product of the Holy Spirit and not generated by the Christian. We need to see the fruit of the Holy Spirit as the very character of God. It is who God is and not just what God does. The fruit manifests first as choices and not emotions, although emotions will be affected. Notice that Paul uses the singular word "fruit" and not the fruits of the Holy Spirit. It is like us looking at the seed of an apple and not the seeds of the apple. It signifies the wholeness of the character of God the Father. Each believer receives all nine fruit as a whole when the Holy Spirit enters at the point of salvation. When we say that we mature as believers, we are developing in the characteristics of God. We are becoming less like us in our sinful ways and more like the Father in His nature. The presence of the "fruit of the Spirit" is evidence that we have experienced genuine salvation, and our character is becoming more like our Lord Jesus Christ.

The Fruit of the Spirit: Defined and Explained.

1. LOVE:

In Gal.5:22-23, the first fruit mentioned is LOVE. This love is from the Greek word agape. As we listed in the study earlier, the Greeks had multiple words for love. The four listed below are all conditional worldly loves that all people operate at different times and degrees.

1. Phileo: Brotherly love
2. Eros: Romantic or erotic sensual love
3. Epithumia: Desire or lust
4. Storge: Old shoe, comfortable love

God's agape love is the unconditional love of God. Real, biblical love is a choice, not a feeling. It deliberately expresses itself by seeking the welfare of others over ourselves. Only Christians can receive this love and are commanded to love God and others with it. God's love at work in us seeks the best for others around us. Biblical love is dependent on God's character, not the emotion of the one receiving it. Again, this is more than what God does; it is who He is. God is love.

1 John 4:8 (ESV) Anyone who does not love does not know God, because God is love.

1 John 4:16 (ESV) So we have come to know and to believe the love that God has for us. God is love, and whoever abides in love abides in God, and God abides in him.

We love God because He first loved us.

1 John 4:19 (ESV) We love because he first loved us.

Love is the most excellent fruit. By the way, some would call love a gift, and that is not only unscriptural, but it is also dangerous. Suppose we decide to be unloving and tell people that we do not have to love because it is not our spiritual gift. Again, Paul said that we do not do anything but love; we have done it all. Manifesting the love of God is proof that we have been born again.

> *1 John 4:7-8 (ESV) Beloved, let us love one another, for love is from God, and whoever loves has been born of God and knows God. 8 Anyone who does not love does not know God, because God is love.*
>
> *1 Corinthians 13:13 (ESV) So now faith, hope, and love abide, these three; but the greatest of these is love.*

God's love should be the expression of The faith we walk. The love of the Father fulfills the law of God. It is the love of God within us that testifies to the world that we are disciples of the Father.

> *Galatians 5:5-6 (ESV) For through the Spirit, by faith, we ourselves eagerly wait for the hope of righteousness. 6 For in Christ Jesus neither circumcision nor uncircumcision counts for anything, but only faith working through love.*
>
> *Romans 13:8-10 (ESV) Owe no one anything, except to love each other, for the one who loves another has fulfilled the law. 9 For the commandments, "You shall not commit adultery, You shall not murder, You shall not steal, You shall not covet," and any other commandment, are summed up in this word: "You shall love your neighbor as yourself." 10 Love does no wrong to a neighbor; therefore love is the fulfilling of the law.*

> *John 13:34-35 (ESV) A new commandment I give to you, that you love one another: just as I have loved you, you also are to love one another. 35 By this all people will know that you are my disciples, if you have love for one another."*

2. JOY:

Joy in Gal.5:22-23 is the Greek word Chara, often translated as joy, delight, or gladness. It maintains the mindset of realizing God's eternal favor and grace in one's life instead of the circumstances surrounding us. It is a feeling of gladness and happiness based on our standing in the Lord that is not dependent on the circumstances surrounding us. Again, this results from a choice we make and not how we feel, even though feelings follow the choice. Even in trials, persecutions, and testing, James tells us to count it all joy.

> *James 1:2-3 (ESV) Count it all joy, my brothers, when you meet trials of various kinds, 3 for you know that the testing of your faith produces steadfastness.*

Paul tells us to rejoice in our sufferings. Would God ask us to do something He did not empower us to fulfill?

> *Romans 5:2-5 (ESV) Through him we have also obtained access by faith into this grace in which we stand, and we rejoice in hope of the glory of God. 3 Not only that, but we rejoice in our sufferings, knowing that suffering produces endurance, 4 and endurance produces character, and character produces hope, 5 and hope does not put us to shame, because God's love has been*

poured into our hearts through the Holy Spirit who has been given to us.

3. PEACE:

The Biblical Greek word for peace is Eirene and carries the concept of a medical term meaning wholeness and harmony with God and others. It is like breaking an arm, and it heals over, becoming stronger at the point of the break. Adam and Eve walked in peace with God. Their sin broke that relationship and that position of peace. Our Lord Jesus Christ came to restore that broken relationship between God and humanity by giving His life a sacrifice to pay for the penalty of sin.

The relationship we have with the Father through the Lord Jesus Christ is healed and stronger than Adam and Eve enjoyed. A life of peace in the Lord is safe and secure, both physically and mentally.

Romans 5:1 (ESV) Therefore, since we have been justified by faith, we have peace with God through our Lord Jesus Christ.

The world does not offer peace because the world cannot give what it does not have or know of.

John 14:27 (ESV) Peace I leave with you; my peace I give to you. Not as the world gives do I give to you. Let not your hearts be troubled, neither let them be afraid.

Peace is a result of allowing the Holy Spirit to work in our hearts and minds. When Christ entered the boat with the disciples, He knew a storm would arise and cause the disciples to fear. However, He brought His pillow to sleep.

He was at peace with the Father in all situations. When we as believers walk in the Spirit, the fruit of peace fills us with inner peace regardless of the storms around us. True Biblical peace is knowing that and walking in the assurance of being reconciled with God.

> *Mark 4:35-40 (ESV) On that day, when evening had come, he said to them, "Let us go across to the other side." 36 And leaving the crowd, they took him with them in the boat, just as he was. And other boats were with him. 37 And a great windstorm arose, and the waves were breaking into the boat, so that the boat was already filling. 38 But he was in the stern, asleep on the cushion. And they woke him and said to him, "Teacher, do you not care that we are perishing?" 39 And he awoke and rebuked the wind and said to the sea, "Peace! Be still!" And the wind ceased, and there was a great calm. 40 He said to them, "Why are you so afraid? Have you still no faith?"*

When we still our hearts in God's peace, we are free from fear and worry about finances, safety, family, health, and salvation. Jesus was hours away from the cross, and he said this in John 16 to encourage his followers.

> *John 16:33 (ESV) I have said these things to you, that in me you may have peace. In the world you will have tribulation. But take heart; I have overcome the world."*

Paul tells us how to think and renew the mind to stay in the position of God's peace. Being anxious is an emotion, and many of us would say that we have no control over it. However, we are commanded not to fear and not to be anxious. Again, God would not tell us to do something if we were not empowered to fulfill it.

> ***Philippians 4:4-9 (ESV)   Rejoice in the Lord always; again I will say, rejoice. 5 Let your reasonableness be known to everyone. The Lord is at hand; 6 do not be anxious about anything, but in everything by prayer and supplication with thanksgiving let your requests be made known to God. 7 And the peace of God, which surpasses all understanding, will guard your hearts and your minds in Christ Jesus. 8 Finally, brothers, whatever is true, whatever is honorable, whatever is just, whatever is pure, whatever is lovely, whatever is commendable, if there is any excellence, if there is anything worthy of praise, think about these things.   9   What you have learned and received and heard and seen in me—practice these things, and the God of peace will be with you.***

4. PATIENCE

Forbearance is not a word that most of us would commonly use. The Greek word for forbearance relates to two words that mean "long and passion," and often translated using other words such as patience, steadfastness, perseverance, longsuffering, and slowness in avenging wrongs. We do not see much patience in the world today, not on the roadways, shopping malls, and even within the church. Since it is a fruit of the Holy Spirit, we would think that Christians would be more longsuffering with one another. Our Lord Jesus Christ through us causes us to be "long-tempered" rather than "short-tempered." Paul used this word when he was describing Jesus' patience with him.

> ***1 Timothy 1:16 (ESV)   But I received mercy for this reason, that in me, as the foremost, Jesus Christ might***

display his perfect patience as an example to those who were to believe in him for eternal life.

Like the Apostle Paul, we all have benefited thankfully from Christ's immense patience with us. The evidence of the Holy Spirit indwelling us is our ability to be patient, steadfast, and long-tempered towards one another. As we read Eph.4:1-3, marvel at how many of the fruit of the Holy Spirit in just one section of Scriptures command us to walk out the Spirit-filled life.

Ephesians 4:1-3 (ESV) I therefore, a prisoner for the Lord, urge you to walk in a manner worthy of the calling to which you have been called, 2 with all humility and gentleness, with patience, bearing with one another in love, 3 eager to maintain the unity of the Spirit in the bond of peace.

5. KINDNESS

Kindness conveys the meaning of moral goodness, integrity, usefulness. The KJV translates this word as "gentleness," which links it to the definition of a gentleman or a gentlewoman. This gentleperson is someone who behaves correctly, with moral integrity and kindness. Put this together, and we have someone who possesses moral goodness and integrity and generously expresses it in the way they act toward others. It is goodness in action.

It was God's kindness that led us to repentance. The Holy Spirit enables us to have moral integrity with kindness and not get trapped in self-righteous judgment. When we show the same kindness to others who need God's salvation, the Holy Spirit has an opportunity to use it to woo their heart to salvation.

> *Romans 2:4 (ESV) Or do you presume on the riches of his kindness and forbearance and patience, not knowing that God's kindness is meant to lead you to repentance?*
>
> *Titus 3:4-5 (ESV) But when the goodness and loving kindness of God our Savior appeared, 5 he saved us, not because of works done by us in righteousness, but according to his own mercy, by the washing of regeneration and renewal of the Holy Spirit,*
>
> *Ephesians 2:7 (ESV) so that in the coming ages he might show the immeasurable riches of his grace in kindness toward us in Christ Jesus.*

One way we know if we are walking in kindness is to evaluate if we are walking in forgiveness.

> *Ephesians 4:31-32 (ESV) Let all bitterness and wrath and anger and clamor and slander be put away from you, along with all malice. 32 Be kind to one another, tenderhearted, forgiving one another, as God in Christ forgave you.*

6. GOODNESS

Goodness means uprightness of heart and life, displaying both God's goodness and kindness. It is like the word righteousness or having the ability to stand right before God. Others can see God's goodness in our actions. This Word relates to being excellent of heart or upright and doing good things in Word, deed, and thought. Through the Holy Spirit's work in the lives of believers, they are upright in heart, and they do good, say, and think good things.

God is good all the time, and His goodness is from everlasting to everlasting. The Word ties the goodness of God to the kingdom of God.

> ***Romans 14:17 (ESV) For the kingdom of God is not a matter of eating and drinking but of righteousness and peace and joy in the Holy Spirit.***

7. FAITHFULNESS

Faithfulness is evidence of the Holy Spirit's work in our lives. To be "faithful" is to be reliable or trustworthy. Faithfulness is a character trait that combines dependability and trust based on our confidence in God and His eternal faithfulness.

In the New Testament, faith is the belief in God and the conviction that Jesus is the Son of God and Savior of humanity through whom we obtain eternal salvation. Christian faithfulness, characterized by continued and consistent submission and obedience to the same Spirit, is also a fruit revealing assurance of salvation. It is the Holy Spirit who provides the ability for us to be faithful. The word "faithful" also describes someone willing to suffer persecution and even face death for Christ's sake.

> ***Hebrews 11:6 (ESV) And without faith it is impossible to please him, for whoever would draw near to God must believe that he exists and that he rewards those who seek him.***

> ***2 Thessalonians 1:4 (ESV) Therefore we ourselves boast about you in the churches of God for your steadfastness and faith in all your persecutions and in the afflictions that you are enduring.***

8. GENTLENESS

Gentleness was translated as "meekness" in the KJV, and modern translations of the Bible use gentleness to mean meekness or mildness of disposition. Meekness is not weakness but strength or power under God's control. An example would be that of a horse. The dominant horse learns to submit to the gentle nudge of the reins on the bit. Our Lord Jesus Christ describes himself as gentle.

> *Matthew 11:29 (ESV) Take my yoke upon you, and learn from me, for I am gentle and lowly in heart, and you will find rest for your souls.*

We are to use gentleness when correcting our opponents. We have the right and responsibility to correct those caught in sin. However, we are to correct using the Spirit of gentleness.

> *2 Timothy 2:24-25 (ESV) And the Lord's servant must not be quarrelsome but kind to everyone, able to teach, patiently enduring evil, 25 correcting his opponents with gentleness. God may perhaps grant them repentance leading to a knowledge of the truth,*

> *Galatians 6:1 (ESV) Brothers, if anyone is caught in any transgression, you who are spiritual should restore him in a spirit of gentleness. Keep watch on yourself, lest you too be tempted.*

> *1 Peter 3:14-15 (ESV) But even if you should suffer for righteousness' sake, you will be blessed. Have no fear of them, nor be troubled, 15 but in your hearts honor Christ the Lord as holy, always being prepared to make a*

defense to anyone who asks you for a reason for the hope that is in you; yet do it with gentleness and respect,

9. SELF-CONTROL

The last characteristic in Paul's description of the fruit of the Spirit points us back to his list of the "works of the flesh" in Gal.5:19-21. Those of us with the indwelling Holy Spirit have the strength to control our sinful desires and to say "no" to our flesh. Self-control is the ability to control one's body and its sensual appetites and passions, physically and mentally, through the power of the Holy Spirit. Self-control relates to both chastity and sobriety, and particularly moderation in eating and drinking. Self-control is the opposite of the works of the flesh that indulge sensual desires.

> *Galatians 5:16-17 (ESV) But I say, walk by the Spirit, and you will not gratify the desires of the flesh. 17 For the desires of the flesh are against the Spirit, and the desires of the Spirit are against the flesh, for these are opposed to each other, to keep you from doing the things you want to do.*

What is the Purpose of Fruit of the Spirit?

1. The Holy Spirit is the holy presence of God.

The Greek word "Spirit" has multiple meanings, including breath, water, Spirit, or wind. It is most commonly used to describe the holy presence of God on earth. Still, New Testament writers also used this word to describe the wind, other spirits, including angels and demons, water, and even the human Spirit. In Galatians 5:22, the phrase "fruit of the Spirit" explicitly refers to what is given to believers by the Holy Spirit.

As believers in Jesus, Christians have the joy of receiving the indwelling Holy Spirit at the moment of the salvation experience. The Father gives the Person and presence of the Holy Spirit to guide believers, empower them, and bring them to all truth.

2. The Fruit of the Spirit indicates a relationship with Christ.

Ephesians 1:13-14 explains that the Holy Spirit is a deposit or down payment given to believers in Christ that guarantees their relationship with Christ. In Galatians 5, Paul wants to make sure that people know how to spot the evidence of the Holy Spirit in their lives. The result of the Holy Spirit in their lives will be good things like love, joy, peace, kindness, and self-control.

> ***Ephesians 1:13-14 (ESV) In him you also, when you heard the word of truth, the gospel of your salvation, and believed in him, were sealed with the promised Holy Spirit, 14 who is the guarantee of our inheritance until we acquire possession of it, to the praise of his glory.***

Paul wants to make sure Christians know that evil actions like sexual immorality, impurity and debauchery; idolatry and witchcraft; hatred, discord, jealousy, fits of rage, selfish ambition, dissensions, factions and envy; drunkenness, orgies are not the work of the Holy Spirit. The fruits of flesh reveal that a person does not know God and does not possess true salvation, no matter how sincere they are confessing that they are born again. In contrast, the fruits of the Holy Spirit are evidence of the work of the Holy Spirit in the lives of Christians.

> *1 Corinthians 6:9-11 (ESV) Or do you not know that the unrighteous will not inherit the kingdom of God? Do not be deceived: neither the sexually immoral, nor idolaters, nor adulterers, nor men who practice homosexuality, 10 nor thieves, nor the greedy, nor drunkards, nor revilers, nor swindlers will inherit the kingdom of God. 11 And such were some of you. But you were washed, you were sanctified, you were justified in the name of the Lord Jesus Christ and by the Spirit of our God.*

3. **Did our Lord Jesus Christ ever talk about the Fruit of the Spirit?**

Jesus did not use the phrase "fruit of the Spirit," but he often mentioned fruit in his teaching. In John 15:5, Jesus said,

> *John 15:5-8 (ESV) I am the vine; you are the branches. Whoever abides in me and I in him, he it is that bears much fruit, for apart from me you can do nothing. 6 If anyone does not abide in me he is thrown away like a branch and withers; and the branches are gathered, thrown into the fire, and burned. 7 If you abide in me, and my words abide in you, ask whatever you wish, and it will be done for you. 8 By this my Father is glorified, that you bear much fruit and so prove to be my disciples.*

The fruit of the Holy Spirit is evidence of being connected to Christ. It is like tree branches or a grapevine connected to the trunk in order to bear grapes. In Matthew

7:16-20, Jesus warned his followers to be wary of false teachers.

> *Matthew 7:15-20 (ESV) "Beware of false prophets, who come to you in sheep's clothing but inwardly are ravenous wolves. 16 You will recognize them by their fruits. Are grapes gathered from thornbushes, or figs from thistles? 17 So, every healthy tree bears good fruit, but the diseased tree bears bad fruit. 18 A healthy tree cannot bear bad fruit, nor can a diseased tree bear good fruit. 19 Every tree that does not bear good fruit is cut down and thrown into the fire. 20 Thus you will recognize them by their fruits.*

The word "Christian" literally means "little Christ" or "little anointed ones." It is the indwelling of the Person of the Holy Spirit that makes this a reality within us. The fruit of the Holy Spirit, also known as the character of God, is within each of us that possesses true salvation, meaning that we are being made Christ-like. As we do what John the Baptist proclaimed, we will witness Christ manifested more within and through us. We need to decrease so that He increases for His glory.

> *John 3:30 (ESV) He must increase, but I must decrease."*

SECTION 4

GOD'S MASTER PLAN OF SALVATION

Chapter 12
HOW TO BECOME A CHRISTIAN:

REMEMBER:
PRAYERS DON'T SAVE PEOPLE:
JESUS SAVES PEOPLE.

The first thing that must happen before people can receive God's redemptive salvation is to realize that they are lost. It is no use in throwing a life preserver to people in the ocean when they are just swimming. They will think that we are crazy. However, if people are drowning, they seriously need and will welcome life preservers.

If people desire to become Christian, known as "being saved" or "to be born again," they need to realize their life requires help and the need of salvation that only exists outside of themselves.

1. Recognize God's love

God loves us. We may not feel it or believe it, but know this, God, the Creator of the heavens and earth, loves us. He loved us enough to give His Son as a sacrifice for the penalty of our sins. We owe a sin debt that we cannot pay, and He paid a sin debt that He did not owe. The love of God makes possible the salvation of humanity.

> *John 3:16-17 (ESV) "For God so loved the world, that he gave his only Son, that whoever believes in him should not perish but have eternal life. 17 For God did not send his Son into the world to condemn the world, but in order that the world might be saved through him.*

2. Recognize that man is lost, separated from God, and cannot save himself through any good works

We cannot and will not come to God on our own accord. This coming to God means that it is the Holy Spirit that woos us and draws us to the heart of the Father. The Holy Spirit convicts or convinces us of three things, and if we do not have this conviction, then the Holy Spirit is not drawing us at the moment. Without the Holy Spirit's work in the conversion process, we risk the danger of just having a mental assent decision of the head without a heart of faith. If the Holy Spirit is drawing us to salvation, there must be a conviction or realization of three things.

1) That we are sinners, and therefore, we cannot save ourselves.

2) Because we are sinners, we will die in our sins, be judged, and spend eternity in hell.

3) That Jesus Christ is both God and the Son of God, died on a cross for our sins, rose from the dead, and is the only way, a person can be saved and escape the judgment of hell.

John 16:8-11 (ESV) And when he comes, he will convict the world concerning sin and righteousness and judgment: 9 concerning sin, because they do not believe in me; 10 concerning righteousness, because I go to the Father, and you will see me no longer; 11 concerning judgment, because the ruler of this world is judged.

3. Recognition of our sin condition:

We must admit that we are sinners. We spend much effort trying to minimize sin and renaming it to make it sound not so condemning. God hates sin, but God loves the sinner. We must approach sin with a more intense attitude than us, "just making a mistake." Mistakes did not send Jesus to the cross. Our sin and our sin nature sent Jesus to the cross. The Bible states that there is no one good except God. People do "good deeds," but their heart is not good. There was only one man who never sinned and could not sin, and that was the Lord Jesus Christ. The rest of humanity stands guilty before a holy God.

> *Romans 3:23 (ESV) for all have sinned and fall short of the glory of God,*
>
> *Luke 18:18-19 (ESV) And a ruler asked him, "Good Teacher, what must I do to inherit eternal life?" 19 And Jesus said to him, "Why do you call me good? No one is good except God alone.*
>
> *Romans 3:10-12 (ESV) as it is written: "None is righteous, no, not one; 11 no one understands; no one seeks for God. 12 All have turned aside; together they have become worthless; no one does good, not even one."*
>
> *1 John 1:8-10 (ESV) If we say we have no sin, we deceive ourselves, and the truth is not in us. 9 If we confess our sins, he is faithful and just to forgive us our sins and to cleanse us from all unrighteousness. 10 If we say we have not sinned, we make him a liar, and his word is not in us.*

4. **Recognize the consequences of sin: The wages of sin is death:**

Unless we recognize our sinful state and change, we will die in our sins, and our souls will be eternally lost.

> *Romans 6:23 (ESV) For the wages of sin is death, but the free gift of God is eternal life in Christ Jesus our Lord.*

5. **Salvation is free to all who believe and is not dependent upon merit of any kind, self-works, or self-worth:**

The good news is that the gift is free and accessible to all who will believe, and it cannot be earned by turning over a new leaf, denying ourselves, or by any good works we might perform.

> *Ephesians 2:8-9 (ESV) For by grace you have been saved through faith. And this is not your own doing; it is the gift of God, 9 not a result of works, so that no one may boast.*

> *Matthew 18:14 (ESV) So it is not the will of my Father who is in heaven that one of these little ones should perish.*

> *Romans 6:23 (ESV) For the wages of sin is death, but the free gift of God is eternal life in Christ Jesus our Lord.*

> *Titus 3:4-7 (ESV) But when the goodness and loving kindness of God our Savior appeared, 5 he saved us, not because of works done by us in righteousness, but according to his own mercy, by the washing of regeneration and renewal of the Holy Spirit, 6 whom he poured out on us richly through Jesus Christ our Savior, 7 so that being justified by his grace we might become heirs according to the hope of eternal life.*

6. **Recognize the sacrifice of Jesus Christ for all humanity.**

Christ's blood paid a debt we could never pay.

Hebrews 9:22 (ESV) Indeed, under the law almost everything is purified with blood, and without the shedding of blood there is no forgiveness of sins.

Hebrews 9:25-26 (ESV) Nor was it to offer himself repeatedly, as the high priest enters the holy places every year with blood not his own, 26 for then he would have had to suffer repeatedly since the foundation of the world. But as it is, he has appeared once for all at the end of the ages to put away sin by the sacrifice of himself.

7. **Believe God and receive the Lord Jesus Christ by grace through faith:**

No man can save himself. We ultimately need the Lord Jesus Christ, who is the Savior of the world. To believe in God means that we also believe in His Word. God's Word is just as true today as it was a million years ago in heaven. The Bible says that Jesus is the Word and came to take on man's flesh for a season and then return to heaven. If we cannot believe that God can preserve His Word through the generations, how can we trust Him to preserve our souls for eternity? To "believe" does not carry some light "so-so," meaning as if something might happen or it might not happen, like the phrase "I believe it might rain." The Biblical Word to "Believe" means to put your total trust in and to place your whole life into the hands of God.

Acts 16:30-31 (ESV) Then he brought them out and said, "Sirs, what must I do to be saved?" 31 And they said, "Believe in the Lord Jesus, and you will be saved, you and your household."

Romans 10:9-10 (ESV) because, if you confess with your mouth that Jesus is Lord and believe in your heart that God raised him from the dead, you will be saved. 10 For with the heart one believes and is justified, and with the mouth one confesses and is saved.

Ephesians 2:8-9 (ESV) For by grace you have been saved through faith. And this is not your own doing; it is the gift of God, 9 not a result of works, so that no one may boast.

Hebrews 11:6 (ESV) And without faith it is impossible to please him, for whoever would draw near to God must believe that he exists and that he rewards those who seek him.

8. **Repent: Make a willful decision to turn away from sin.**

Becoming a Christian is not just about receiving Jesus as Savior and then continuing life as usual. Becoming a Christian is a life exchange. We give Him our broken down depraved, sinful life, and He gives us a new life, the life of God. He makes us a new person in Him. This change is what we call repentance. It is doing an about-face and going in the opposite direction. It is to feel regret for sin, a change in our mind, and a turning from sin to God. We demonstrate the change in our hearts by our actions in word, deed, and thought.

> *Luke 13:3 (ESV) No, I tell you; but unless you repent, you will all likewise perish.*

> *Acts 20:20-21 (ESV) how I did not shrink from declaring to you anything that was profitable, and teaching you in public and from house to house, 21 testifying both to Jews and to Greeks of repentance toward God and of faith in our Lord Jesus Christ.*

Confession of sin is a fruit of repentance, and it brings to light those deeds that keep us in bondage.

> *1 John 1:9 (ESV) If we confess our sins, he is faithful and just to forgive us our sins and to cleanse us from all unrighteousness.*

> *James 5:16 (ESV) Therefore, confess your sins to one another and pray for one another, that you may be healed. The prayer of a righteous person has great power as it is working.*

9. Be converted. Also known as being "born again."

This new life is what God does for us when we call upon the Name of our Lord Jesus Christ to save us. This salvation experience is the new birth. It is a miracle of spiritual life performed by the Holy Spirit through faith in the sacrificial, atoning blood of Jesus Christ.

> *Matthew 18:3 (ESV) and said, "Truly, I say to you, unless you turn and become like children, you will never enter the kingdom of heaven.*

> *John 3:3 (ESV) Jesus answered him, "Truly, truly, I say to you, unless one is born again he cannot see the kingdom of God."*

NOW...If we believe the points above, we can pray (call upon) and ask the Lord Jesus Christ to receive our life because we are giving it to Him, and we are receiving His life in us. We need to ask Jesus right now to forgive us. If we do this with a heart of faith, the Bible says that we will be saved and forgiven. We will be known as Christians and children of God. Lord Jesus, forgive us (forgive me).

> *John 1:12 (ESV) But to all who did receive him, who believed in his name, he gave the right to become children of God,*
>
> *John 20:31 (ESV) but these are written so that you may believe that Jesus is the Christ, the Son of God, and that by believing you may have life in his name.*
>
> *John 3:36 (ESV) Whoever believes in the Son has eternal life; whoever does not obey the Son shall not see life, but the wrath of God remains on him.*
>
> *John 5:24 (ESV) Truly, truly, I say to you, whoever hears my word and believes him who sent me has eternal life. He does not come into judgment, but has passed from death to life.*

Chapter 13
THE MASTER PLAN OF EVANGELISM

We know that God has called us to be a bold witness for our Lord Jesus Christ. However, it seems we are losing the battle of soul winning. There are many reasons for someone not sharing Christ. Let us look at a few.

1. We rely on the "paid staff" to witness and win people to Jesus.

2. We fail to get trained in the witnessing process. Therefore, we feel insecure or even fearful of sharing Christ.

3. We embrace bad theology about who will have eternal life and who will be lost. Therefore, we do not see a need to witness.

4. We fail to walk a Holy Spirit-filled life before people; therefore, we feel, who are we to share anything about Christ?

In the master plan of evangelism, we will share some key insights that should make the witnessing experience exciting and filled with high expectations.

POINT # 1: IT IS THE HOLY SPIRIT THAT DRAWS PEOPLE TO CHRIST, NOT US.

If we take the credit, we need to take the blame. However, if we enter the witnessing experience with the full realization that the whole process is a work of the Holy Spirit and we are just vessels to be used by God, we keep the proper perspective.

1. We must pray and believe that the Holy Spirit will precede the witnessing encounter. (Read Acts 10:1-15)

2. We must believe that it is up to the Holy Spirit to reveal God's existence. (Read Romans 1:18-23)

3. We must believe that it is the work of the Holy Spirit to convict or convince of three critical elements of the witnessing process and salvation. (Read John 16:8-11)

    1) The Holy Spirit convicts that we are sinners and therefore lost
    2) The Holy Spirit convicts that Christ is righteous, that He is the Son of God, and God.
    3) The Holy Spirit convicts that judgment is already cast, and we are headed to a devil's hell if we reject God's salvation.

4. We must believe that the Holy Spirit brings a lost person from spiritual death to spiritual life. (Read John 3:5-6; Titus 3:5). Anything else, and we have only a mental assent (head knowledge) conversion where the heart did not exercise faith. This mental assent would be a false salvation experience with false assurance.

5. We must believe that it is the Holy Spirit that empowers the one who is doing the witnessing. (Read Acts 1:4, 8; Luke 24:49)

1) The Holy Spirit empowers with authority in the witnessing process. (Read Matthew 28:18-20)
2) The Holy Spirit empowers with boldness in the witnessing process. (Read Acts 4:30-31)
3) The Holy Spirit empowers with wisdom in the witnessing process. (Read Luke 12:12)

One of the methods proven effective in witnessing is using what is called "The Romans Road to Salvation." We started memorizing the Romans Road Scriptures back in 1974 and used them extensively in soul winning.

Remember that there are three keys ingredients in witnessing that cannot be ignored. The first is the work of the Holy Spirit. Winning someone to Jesus is, first and foremost, the work of the Holy Spirit. The second is the Word of God. Faith comes by hearing and hearing by the Word of God. (Read Rom.10:17). This need for people to hear the Word is why we are using the Romans Road Scriptures. The third ingredient is our testimony. Our salvation testimony carries authority and power.

We have a sin problem. Our problem extends beyond the fact that we are sinners because we sin. It is better to say that we sin because we are sinners. We have a sin-nature problem in that our family conceived us in iniquity just like their parents did and so forth. We were born with the seed to sin, and as soon as we could, we manifested sin. Do we wonder why children learn the word "no" first? We do not have to teach children how to have bad behavior; they already have that within them. We have to teach them morality and ethical behavior. We tried teaching our small children how to eat out of their bowls. However, they always seemed to throw it on the floor. We did not teach them to throw their food on the floor. That sinful nature was already in them to do that.

ROMANS ROAD CHART:

God is holy, and humanity is sinful. Therefore, there is a great gulf separating the two. That gulf is the sinfulness of humanity. The fact that no one is righteous is stated in <u>**Romans 3:10-12.**</u> Also noted is the fact that we do not nor will not seek after God. It is God through the Holy Spirit that comes seeking after us. In <u>**Romans 3:23,**</u> we find a passage that is speaking about an event in a sporting contest. The event is archery. The target represents the glory of God. We cannot hit the target or even come close. Our arrows fall short before getting close to the target. We find in <u>**Romans 6:23**</u> the consequences of our sin and sin nature are physical and spiritual death.

Most people have a preference for Bible translations. We cannot list the Romans Road Scriptures in every translation. Therefore, we will limit it to three of the most prominently used translations, *the King James Version* (KJV), *the American Standard Version* (ASV), and *the English Standard Version* (ESV).

1. **We are sinners, and there is no good in us. Romans 3:10-12; 3:23; 6:23.**

KJV	ASV	ESV
ROM.3:10-12 KJV	**ROM.3:10-12 ASV**	**ROM.3:10-12 ESV**
As it is written, There is none righteous, no, not	as it is written, there is none righteous, no, not	as it is written: "None is righteous, no, not one; 11 no

one: 11 There is none that understandeth, there is none that seeketh after God. 12 They are all gone out of the way, they are together become unprofitable; there is none that doeth good, no, not one.	one; 11 there is none that understandeth, there is none that seeketh after god; 12 they have all turned aside, they are together become unprofitable; there is none that doeth good, no, not so much as one:	one understands; no one seeks for God. 12 All have turned aside; together they have become worthless; no one does good, not even one."
ROM.3:23 KJV	**ROM.3:23 ASV**	**ROM.3:23 ESV**
For all have sinned, and come short of the glory of God;	for all have sinned, and fall short of the glory of God;	for all have sinned and fall short of the glory of God,
ROM.6:23 KJV	**ROM.6:23 ASV**	**ROM.6:23 ESV**
For the wages of sin is death; but the gift of God is eternal life through Jesus Christ our Lord.	For the wages of sin is death; but the free gift of God is eternal life in Christ Jesus our Lord.	For the wages of sin is death, but the free gift of God is eternal life in Christ Jesus our Lord.

2. God has a plan, and we have hope.

God had a plan for humanity before the foundation of the world. If we stayed in our sins, we would be hopeless. However, God's plan was in place before He created man. We have been given hope through the free gift of salvation. God did this by His love for us (*John 3:16*) by His grace, which is unearned or unmerited favor (*Ephesians 2:8:9*). The hope we have is eternal life in and through our Lord Jesus

Christ. The second part of **_Romans 6:23_** reveals that God made a plan before He made man that we have the right to eternal life. We find that eternal life only in the Lord Jesus Christ and His work on the cross.

In **_Romans 5:8_**, we see that the cross is always present tense. When Christ was on the cross, He demonstrated His love for us as if Christ died on the cross today just for us and for our salvation. He knew us before He created us. This plan of God for the redemption of humanity represents the love of God in a great demonstration.

ROM.6:23 KJV	ROM.6:23 ASV	ROM.6:23 ESV
For the wages of sin is death; but the gift of God is eternal life through Jesus Christ our Lord.	For the wages of sin is death; but the free gift of God is eternal life in Christ Jesus our Lord.	For the wages of sin is death, but the free gift of God is eternal life in Christ Jesus our Lord.

ROM.5:8 KJV	ROM.5:8 ASV	ROM.5:8 ESV
But God commendeth his love toward us, in that, while we were yet sinners, Christ died for us.	But God commendeth his own love toward us, in that, while we were yet sinners, Christ died for us.	but God shows his love for us in that while we were still sinners, Christ died for us.

3. We must respond to God's great invitation and gift.

We have made and will continue to make decisions throughout our lives, hoping that they will be in our best interest. Most of us can point to a decision or two or action in our past and say that we wish we had not made it, and we regretted the outcome. The same is valid with the free gift of salvation offered by our Lord Jesus Christ. It would seem to many of us as a "no-brainer" decision. Do we receive Christ and have our lives changed, sins are forgiven, and have eternal life with God in His kingdom forever? Or do we reject Christ, try to maintain our current life status, die in our sins, and spend eternity in hell separated from God and all that is godly? We know, to some, they would say it is not that simple, but really, it is. It is a choice we make for Christ by faith to receive His work on the cross and repent (turn away from) our sinful nature and sinful ways. However, how does someone do this? It is a confession of the mouth and a belief of the heart, which we find in **_Rom.10:9-10_** and **_10:13_**. This third stage is a calling out to Jesus to receive His salvation.

ROM.10:9-10 KJV	ROM.10:9-10 ASV	ROM.10:9-10 ESV
That if thou shalt confess with thy mouth the Lord Jesus, and shalt believe in thine heart that God hath raised him from the dead, thou shalt be saved.	because if thou shalt confess with thy mouth Jesus as Lord, and shalt believe in thy heart that God raised him from the dead, thou shalt be saved:	because, if you confess with your mouth that Jesus is Lord and believe in your heart that God raised him from the dead, you will be saved.
For with the heart man believeth unto righteousness; and with the mouth confession is made unto salvation.	for with the heart man believeth unto righteousness; and with the mouth confession is made unto salvation.	For with the heart one believes and is justified, and with the mouth one confesses and is saved.
ROM.10:13 KJV	ROM.10:13 ASV	ROM.10:13 ESV

| For whosoever shall call upon the name of the Lord shall be saved. | for, Whosoever shall call upon the name of the Lord shall be saved. | For "everyone who calls on the name of the Lord will be saved." |

4. There is glory in receiving God's grace.

Suppose we lived in a ten-million-dollar home and were chauffeured around in a Rolls-Royce. People everywhere would want to see our home and those on the roadway that would point to our Rolls-Royce and comment. It goes with the territory. If we walk in what we have, we will receive attention and maybe glory. The same is valid with becoming a believer. Only God gets all the glory. He has blessed us, gifted us, and called us His children (Read *<u>1 Corinthians 12-14; John 1:12</u>*). Once receiving our Lord Jesus Christ as Savior, everything changes. We no longer need to fear because, by faith, we have peace with God. (*<u>Romans 5:1-2</u>*).

Because God has forgiven our past, we are no longer under condemnation or the law of sin and death. Sin and the grave are no longer our slave owners and masters. We are free from both. (*<u>Romans 8:1-2</u>*). We are no more classified as sinners but as saints. We may sin, but not called sinners. Just like lost people may do good deeds, but they are not to be called saints. Our status is one of sonship in which we cry out, "Abba, Father." The Greek term "Abba" means daddy. The Holy Spirit within us confirms that we are God's children. (*<u>Romans 8:15-16</u>*)

ROM.5:1 KJV	**ROM.5:1 ASV**	**ROM.5:1 ESV**
Therefore being justified by faith, we have peace with	Being therefore justified by faith, we have peace with	Therefore, since we have been justified by faith, we have

God through our Lord Jesus Christ:	God through our Lord Jesus Christ;	peace with God through our Lord Jesus Christ.

ROM.8:1-2 KJV	**ROM.8:1-2 ASV**	**ROM.8:1-2 ESV**
There is therefore now no condemnation to them which are in Christ Jesus, who walk not after the flesh, but after the Spirit.	There is therefore now no condemnation to them that are in Christ Jesus.	There is therefore now no condemnation for those who are in Christ Jesus.
For the law of the Spirit of life in Christ Jesus hath made me free from the law of sin and death.	For the law of the Spirit of life in Christ Jesus made me free from the law of sin and of death.	For the law of the Spirit of life has set you free in Christ Jesus from the law of sin and death.

ROM.8:15-16 KJV	ROM.8:15-16 ASV	ROM.8:15-16 ESV
For ye have not received the spirit of bondage again to fear; but ye have received the Spirit of adoption, whereby we cry, Abba, Father.	For ye received not the spirit of bondage again unto fear; but ye received the spirit of adoption, whereby we cry, Abba, Father.	For you did not receive the spirit of slavery to fall back into fear, but you have received the Spirit of adoption as sons, by whom we cry, "Abba! Father!"
The Spirit itself beareth witness with our spirit, that we are the children of God:	The Spirit himself beareth witness with our spirit, that we are children of God:	The Spirit himself bears witness with our spirit that we are children of God,

5. Leading someone in prayer for salvation:

As we said earlier, "prayers do not save people; Jesus saves people." Therefore, in the calling out to Christ for salvation, we have to hope and pray that the person praying has a heart of faith. We do an injustice trying to convince someone after they pray "the prayer" that they are a child of God. Tell them that if they prayed in faith, the five witnesses of salvation would be evident in their life. Please do not give them false assurance before the fruit of the Holy Spirit is seen on the tree. Remember that the fruit reveals the root.

Let us get to the prayer stage. We can pray for those who wish to call on our Lord to receive salvation. However, we are praying that their decision is genuine and that they have a heart of faith and repentance. We cannot pray them into salvation. They must call upon the Lord. We should not tell them what to say or have them repeat a prayer after us. If a lost person wishes to receive Christ as Savior, then they are moved by the Holy Spirit to be saved. They will know how to repent and confess what needs to be said. We need to stop trying to play the part of the Holy Spirit in people's lives.

Again, before praying with someone to receive Christ, they need to be asked if they understand and agree with three critical statements.

1) That we are sinners, and we cannot save ourselves.
2) Because we are sinners, we will die in our sins, be judged, and spend eternity in hell.
3) That Jesus Christ is both God and the Son of God, died on a cross for our sins, rose from the dead, and is

the only way a person can be saved and escape the judgment of hell.

If they disagree with any of these, we should not pray with them because only the Holy Spirit brings a person to salvation. Moreover, before salvation happens in a person, the Holy Spirit convicts or convinces the person of sin, righteousness, and judgment. If they do not have these convictions, then the Holy Spirit is not wooing their heart at this time.

Steps to leading someone to Christ:
1. Admit that you are a sinner and that you need God's help.
2. Be willing to change your mind and turn from your sin (repent).
3. Believe that Jesus Christ is the Son of God and God and that He died for you, was buried, and rose from the dead.
4. Through prayer, invite Jesus into your heart to become your personal Lord and Savior.
5. Pray:

These sample prayers should be just that, samples. We can let the lost people read one if they need an idea of how to get started. However, it is the heart of faith that saves a man, not the prayer. We know there will be some who disagree, so let us consider this. What if the person under conviction is mute and cannot pray our prayer, are they lost because they cannot voice our prayer? If you are ready to receive this free gift of God's salvation, pray this **prayer believing with your heart**:

> *Lord Jesus, I confess my sins and ask for your forgiveness. Please come into my heart as my Lord and Savior. I receive your life, and I give you my life. I confess you are Lord and that God raised You from the dead. Help me to walk in Your footsteps daily by the power of the Holy Spirit. I ask this in the name of Jesus Christ.*

> ***Romans 10:9-10** "That if you confess with your mouth, "Jesus is Lord," and believe in your heart that God raised him from the dead, you will be saved. For it is with your heart that you believe and are justified, and it is with your mouth that you confess and are saved."*

Some choose to lead people to pray Psalms 51

> ***Psalms 51:1-13 (ESV)** To the choirmaster. A Psalm of David, when Nathan the prophet went to him, after he had gone in to Bathsheba. Have mercy on me, O God, according to your steadfast love; according to your abundant mercy blot out my transgressions. 2 Wash me thoroughly from my iniquity, and cleanse me from my sin! 3 For I know my transgressions, and my sin is ever before me. 4 Against you, you only, have I sinned and done what is evil in your sight, so that you may be justified in your words and blameless in your judgment. 5 Behold, I was brought forth in iniquity, and in sin did my mother conceive me. 6 Behold, you delight in truth in the inward being, and you teach me wisdom in the secret heart. 7 Purge me with hyssop, and I shall be clean; wash me, and I shall be whiter than snow. 8 Let me hear joy and gladness; let the bones that you have broken rejoice. 9 Hide your face from my sins, and blot out all my iniquities. 10 Create in me a clean heart, O God, and renew a right spirit within me. 11 Cast me not away from your presence, and take not your Holy Spirit*

from me. 12 Restore to me the joy of your salvation, and uphold me with a willing spirit. 13 Then I will teach transgressors your ways, and sinners will return to you.

Chapter 14
RECAP OF THE FIVE WITNESSES OF SALVATION

When we were lost, the Holy Spirit was beside us, working His work to bring us to the place of salvation and righteousness. The pieces of evidence of the Holy Spirit walking beside us prove that God is dealing with us and is calling us to salvation. Those pieces of evidence are conviction of sin, righteousness, and judgment. He said that His Spirit would not always strive with man. This ceasing of the Holy Spirit's conviction means that someone who is lost and experiencing the conviction or wooing of the Holy Spirit today should not assume that the same conviction or wooing will be there tomorrow. We must teach people to respond quickly to the calling of God because today is the day of salvation.

> *2 Corinthians 6:2 ESV For he says, "In a favorable time I listened to you, and in a day of salvation I have helped you." Behold, now is the favorable time; behold, now is the day of salvation.*

> *Hebrews 3:7-8 ESV Therefore, as the Holy Spirit says, "Today, if you hear his voice, (8) do not harden your hearts as in the rebellion, on the day of testing in the wilderness,*

The evidence that the Holy Spirit is beside me: John 16:8-11

1. The revelation of the conviction of sin

2. The revelation of the righteousness of Christ
3. The judgment of God on all who are lost

Once responding to the wooing of the Holy Spirit and accepting by faith the salvation purchased by our Lord Jesus Christ, we are genuinely born again. The Holy Spirit moves from being "beside us" to the position of "within us."

These pieces of evidence that the Holy Spirit dwells within us serve us as proof that we have experienced genuine salvation. This spiritual salvation means that God dwells in us, making us the temple of His presence, and He has given us the right to be called His children. We cannot pick and choose which evidences of salvation we would like to have. All five pieces of evidence must verify proof of salvation.

The five witnesses or shreds of evidence that the Holy Spirit is within me:

1. The **Scriptural Testimony**: The Scriptural witness is the salvation testimony given by the believer.
2. The **Internal Witness**: The Internal witness is the witness of the Holy Spirit with our spirit that we are children of God.
3. The **External Witness**: The External witness is the manifestation of the fruit of the Spirit, also known as the character of God, which reveals a changed life.
4. The **Fraternal Witness**: The Fraternal witness is only evidenced by the love for the brothers and sisters of the faith, revealing the spirit of adoption as children of God.

5. The **Paternal Witness**: The Paternal witness is the correction or chastening of the Lord in our lives when we sin.

Now that we know the five pieces of evidence or proofs of true salvation, we can both examine ourselves to ensure that we are in the faith, and we can also "know them by their fruit."

ABOUT THE AUTHOR

CHARLES is passionate about the manifested presence of God, seeing the Father's authentic Biblical leadership taking their position of grace and authority and working towards seeing true Biblical unity in the Spirit and unity of the faith within the body of Christ. Charles founded Raising the Standard International Ministries (RSIM), assisting pastors, spiritual leaders, and the body of Christ to pursue these key objectives. Charles is known for his uncompromising approach to God's Word without denominational or religious bias. He has the unique ability to use word pictures to paint the truth of God's Word. His message, uncompromising in nature, instills the virtues of honor and respect for other believers, whether they are in a position of authority, being a peer, or being entrusted to shepherding and care. Charles' key message for the believer is one of dying daily to self, embracing the beauty in personal brokenness, and walking in the power of the Holy Spirit.

Made in United States
Orlando, FL
03 January 2025